Road Home

REX OGLE

Norton Young Readers

An Imprint of W. W. Norton & Company
Independent Publishers Since 1923

*To anyone who's ever been pushed away
or disowned for being different.*

For information about permission to reproduce selections from this book, write to Permissions, W. W. Norton & Company, Inc., 500 Fifth Avenue, New York, NY 10110

For information about special discounts for bulk purchases, please contact W. W. Norton Special Sales at specialsales@wwnorton.com or 800-233-4830

Manufacturing by Lakeside Book Company
Book design by Hana Anouk Nakamura
Production manager: Delaney Adams

ISBN 978-1-324-01992-3

W. W. Norton & Company, Inc., 500 Fifth Avenue, New York, N.Y. 10110
www.wwnorton.com

W. W. Norton & Company Ltd., 15 Carlisle Street, London W1D 3BS

1 2 3 4 5 6 7 8 9 0

AUTHOR'S NOTE

What you're about to read is a true story. This is my story. It happened to me.

And as painful as it was for me to write, it may be equally or more painful for you to read—especially if you've lived through something similar. So I want to offer you a warning. This book contains depictions of homelessness, violence, sexual assault, and suicidal ideation.

If you're not ready to read this, please don't. Instead, take care of yourself first. This book will be waiting when you are ready.

But know this: I lived this, and I survived. You survived your past too, or you wouldn't be here reading this. We are both alive. We may have a few more scars than we'd like—inside and out—but we made it through. No matter how dark the past, or even the present, the sun will always come up tomorrow.

———

This story took place during the summer of 1998.

This was before cell phones were a common possession and before the internet was widely available. So it was difficult to reach out to people, and I didn't have online search engines to google for resources. In fact, Google didn't even exist at the time.

That meant I didn't have easy access to resources. I didn't even know a lot of resources existed. At the time, there probably weren't many for LGBTQ youth. But there are now.

If you are experiencing, or someone you know is experiencing, home instability, or dealing with thoughts of suicide, there is help. Please reach out.

The Trevor Project
https://www.thetrevorproject.org
https://www.thetrevorproject.org/resources/article/resources-for-lgbtq-youth-experiencing-homelessness/

988 Suicide and Crisis Hotline
https://988lifeline.org/
Or call 988

Road Home

the beach

The ocean roars in my ears, trying to swallow the happy cries of children running toward, and from, the Pensacola waves. A seagull pecks at the shore, raising its white wings at me, flaps them, then struts away. The sun hangs in the wide blue sky, watching over everything below.

I sit on my towel, toes dug into the sand, taking in the view. I lower my eyes back into my book—until Jill comes along and kicks sand at me with the end of her foot.

"Hey! I'm reading!"

"I know. Which is totally dumb. You're on vacation! Enjoy the beach!"

"People read at the beach."

Jill shakes her head. "Yeah, senior citizens."

"I'm seventeen."

"Then why are you acting like a crotchety old man?" Jill steals my paperback book. She thumbs through it, then looks at the cover. She sticks her tongue out. "*Interview with the Vampire?*"

I try to take it back, but she holds it out of my reach. "Uh-uh. Not until you at least get in the water."

"After this chapter."

Jill takes three steps back, moving toward an incoming wave. "One of you is coming swimming with me, right now. It's either you or Anne Rice."

"Okay!" I hold my hands up in surrender. She hands the book back, and I tuck it carefully into my towel. I don't want it to get wet. Or sand between the pages, which is a hard ask at the beach. I get up, dust myself off. Jill grabs my hand and pulls me toward the water.

I tiptoe in. After the blaring sun, the water is bracing against my feet and ankles. Stepping forward, cold up to my knees, I wait until my body adapts. Until another wave crashes against me, splashing and spotting me with cool drops. I'm done waiting. I dive in. My hot skin breathes a sigh of relief at the crisp fresh feeling. As my head pierces the surface, I inhale the early summer air. Salt water gently burns my eyes.

I run a hand over my shaved head, each hair a sharp bristle against my palm. There's nothing like a fresh crew cut and fade. Especially to look my best for a long weekend with my coworkers, who invited me to join them for their Memorial Day trip to the beach. I don't know Jill or Rich or Karen all that well, but I thought, Why not? It's good to make friends.

And I should live a little before college starts in the fall.

So yesterday we drove down from Prattville, Alabama. Three hours, from a small town to a city on the ocean.

I dive under a wave, and let my momentum carry me. The water is blue, almost green, murky with particles everywhere. But the water feels like home. Like when I was three and we lived in Okinawa and Guam. My dad was stationed there for the Air Force. We lived on a beach. I would wade out into the water and just float. My first memories are of water.

Just floating.

Rich splashes me. "The water is perfect. Why didn't you come in sooner?"

I shrug, awkward, trying not to look at Rich without his shirt on. His muscular chest rises just above the water. His body hair wet, gleaming. He smiles, and a small crush aches inside me. Even when Karen leaps on his back and ducks him and they come up kissing. Karen is nice, and I like them together. I wish I had someone to duck and wrestle and splash with. To kiss.

But I'm perpetually single. Mostly, I always have been. I had girlfriends in junior high and high school. But they never lasted.

Jumping straight into a wave, I drift under the surface, using cupped hands to propel me forward. The shark from *Jaws* comes to mind, but I push that image away. I punch up into the air, one arm pulling me after the other, following through, swimming out farther and farther, where the waves rise higher, where I can't touch the shifting floor. Jill follows, then so do Karen and Rich. Our heads bob up and down like apples in a barrel of water.

We talk about work. About the blue vests we're required to wear. About pushing shopping carts, stocking shelves, how we each manage to get out of cleaning the bathrooms. There's nothing worse than cleaning the public bathrooms at Walmart. We laugh at the mere thought of the smells and sights that await us.

After a while, the others get tired and head back to shore.

But I'm enjoying myself too much. The waves raising me up and letting me down, up and down, again and again.

I can't touch the bottom here. It's too deep. But I'm a good swimmer. Good at treading water. So I tread. Holding myself steady at the crests of the tall waves.

From here, I look back at the beach. The land goes on and on in either direction. Tiny rectangles of blankets and towels. Circles of umbrellas. Adults and children tanning, building sandcastles, putting on sunscreen, throwing footballs and Frisbees. In the water, people swim, ride floats, call out "Marco" and "Polo."

The farther you go out, the less people there are.

This far out, it's just me.

Turning my head the other way, I watch the waves ebb and flow, washing toward me, as if bringing me a message. I can't see the end of the ocean. It just goes on, out of sight, to unknown depths, as if toward oblivion.

I can't help but think about the last book I read in high school. Kate Chopin's *The Awakening*. It ends with a woman swimming out into the Gulf of Mexico, never intending to come back.

A dull ache rises inside me. I'm not sure if it's from being made to feel small, or being made to feel like I'm part of the whole thing. I spin myself in the water, watching the horizon. The sea draws on, until it meets land, and the land becomes water again. The world wraps itself around me, going in a circle forever.

I don't know how long I'm out here. Alone. Just floating, where the sky meets the sea.

After a long while, laughter rises up behind me. A group of guys race out. They splash at each other. Chatting in a friendly manner. But I can't hear what they're saying over there. I'm too distracted. One of them keeps glancing over at me. Smiling.

A wave splashes me in the face, pushes me under.

I come back up. And he's still watching me. Staring.

I find myself staring back. I can't help it.

There's some vibration between us. A chemistry. I can't label it. It's too raw. Too natural. And at the same time, forbidden.

The guy smiles again at me, from thirty feet away. Pink lips. Blue eyes. A mole on his right cheek. Short dirty blond hair. He's busy looking at me when a wave hits him. He comes up laughing.

Letting the waves raise me up, drop me low, I'm still treading water. Trying not to be too obvious. His friends turn back, swimming toward the shore. I'm waiting for my viewer to go after his friends. But he doesn't. One of his buddies calls out, "You coming?"

"In a minute," he calls back, never taking his eyes off me. Like he knows something, something about me, something I'm trying to hide. And I can't look away.

Just the two of us, out here among the waves.

"Perfect beach day, huh?" he calls out in a thick southern drawl.

Feeling my face flush red, I hesitate to speak. Before it gets awkward, I call out, "Yeah." Hoping he can't see me blushing under my fresh sunburn.

He keeps looking at me. Keeps smiling at me. No one else is near.

He swims a little closer, maybe twenty feet away.

"What's your name?" he asks.

"Rex."

"Rex," he repeats. Still smirking. "I thought that was a dog's name."

"You're not the first person to say that."

"Rawrf!" he barks. Then he barks again, more real this time. Like a beagle. Then he howls. He laughs. "I'm just joshing you. It's a good name."

"Thanks."

He says, "I'm Russell." He waves from ten feet away. "Nice to meet you."

"You too."

I don't know what else to say. Water splashes me. I take a mouthful and spit it at him. Not aggressively. Just playful. He spits water back at me.

Words fail me as I try to talk. I think I see a fish tail in the distance. "Ever see *Little Mermaid*?" I ask, thinking of the Disney heroine who makes a deal with a witch to transform into something new, something better, for the love of a prince she hardly knows. Then I realize how dumb it is to bring up a kids' cartoon to a total stranger. A handsome stranger. And how pointed it is to bring up a story about love. "Sorry. That was a stupid question."

He shakes his head. "It's okay that you're stupid. I like being the smart one."

"I doubt you're that smart," I say. Then I worry I've offended him. But I didn't. I know cause he's laughing.

"You're cute," he says.

A huge wave punches me in the face, pushes me under. I'm glad for it. Cause when I come up, I can't speak. Paranoid, I look around. I check back at the beach. Jill and Rich and Karen now at our towels, I breathe this heavy sigh of relief. Cause they don't know. Cause nobody knows. Knows about me, the real me, here in Alabama. Maybe my stepsister, cause I've dropped hints. But I haven't said it. Not out loud.

Why would I? I'm not even sure I am.

In junior high I thought, maybe. I'd had so many crushes. But on girls and guys. And I told a few close friends. They said I might be. But I didn't want that label. I didn't want to be . . .

You know.

Gay.

"Sorry," Russell says, his grin gone. His eyes have a touch of uncertainty, like he might swim away. "I didn't mean to—"

"No, it's okay." But I feel some of my strength gone. Like my legs can't kick forever. Like my arms might give out. I'm still looking around. Making sure no one is close.

Russell closes the distance between us to five feet. I tread back a little. Scared.

He asks, "Are you . . . ?"

"I don't know." I ask, "Are you?"

He smiles and nods. "Yup. Gay as the sky is blue."

I hesitate. But no one is near. Just me, Russell, and thoughts of *Little Mermaid* and Kate Chopin. Finally, I say, "Cool."

He swims closer. Four feet. Then three.

The ocean has never felt this small.

Two feet.

One.

Looking at his lips makes everything in me go sideways. My body warm. Full of something new, unfamiliar, but in the best way. Under the water, his hand reaches out and grazes mine. He smiles. I smile back. He leans in.

I swim back two feet. Three. Four. Five. Looking back to

the beach, I see Jill's hand is over her eyes, like she's trying to see out here.

"I . . . I can't," I say, swimming back farther. Six feet. Seven. Eight. "I'm sorry. I just . . . I can't.

"Can't what?"

"I don't know," I say. And then I'm swimming back to shore. Even as I'm thinking about Russell's lips, his eyes, the way he barked at me. I swim faster and faster until I'm walking out of the sea, up the beach, sand caking my feet, to the towels.

"What did that guy want?" Jill asks. With one hand, she holds the small golden cross attached to the slender chain around her neck.

I look back to Russell. I don't see him anymore. There are too many heads bobbing in the water. And no one is out there that far anymore.

"He just wanted to know what time it was," I say.

Jill looks at my wrists. "But you don't have a watch."

"Right," I say. "That's what I told him."

———

We go back to the hotel room and shower. Jill goes first. Then Rich and Karen go together, laughing the whole time behind the door. Jill shakes her head.

After the others have showered, I go last. My skin almost crimson, kissed by the sun. But that's not what fills my head. I'm drunk with thoughts of Russell. His laugh. The touch of his hand. His lips as he leaned in.

I try to push him out of my mind.

I could have, but I didn't.

And now he's gone.

Forever.

An ache fills up inside me, like I lost something of value. Like I missed my chance at winning something. Gaining something important. Not being alone.

Even as I slip back into dry clothes. Even as we go to dinner at a Tex-Mex restaurant. Even as Jill and Rich and Karen laugh. Even as Rich buys two six-packs of Zima, and we go back to our hotel room and sit on the balcony and drink until I feel fuzzy. Even still, all I can see is Russell, smirking in the water at me. Why didn't I . . . ?

Why am I so scared all the time?

Is it cause I grew up in Texas? Cause I saw other maybe-gay boys get beat up? Cause I got called a homo and a faggot? Cause since I was little I got pushed around, even though I insisted I was straight? Cause my whole family's Christian? Church of Christ on my mom's side. Southern Baptist on my dad's. Cause being gay is a sin? Cause I don't want to burn in hell? I don't even know if I believe in god or heaven or hell. I don't know what I believe. I don't even know what I am.

I've liked girls. But I've liked boys too. In secret.

So what am I?

————

Rich and Karen share a bed, Rich wrapped around her like Velcro. Jill and I share the other full-sized mattress. She places two pillows in between us, saying, "Let's pretend Jesus is sleeping in the middle."

But I can't sleep. I feel like I'm still in the ocean. Still rising and falling. Up and down. Dizzy almost. Like I'm seasick, but on land. The vertigo is too strong with my eyes closed. So I get up gently, quietly, to slip on my flip-flops, grab my book, and sneak out.

The hotel is huge. It's the nicest place I've ever stayed. Though that's not saying much. I've never stayed anywhere but Holiday Inns with my family on road trips. The walls rise up twenty feet, to a painted mural on the ceiling. The lobby here goes on and on. The checkout desk, the elevator bank, the bar with people still partying. All of it with tanned columns, details of turquoise, and brightly flowered wallpaper. Then there's a small nook, a sitting area with red carpet, nice chairs, and shelves full of books. No one's here. I look around, as if I need permission. No one notices me. So I take a seat.

I open my own book, about a lonely vampire. And I read the same sentence fourteen times. I can't focus. Cause all I'm thinking about is the ocean. About Russell. About him barking without a care. Smiling at me. *Me.* I feel the corners of my lips turn up, and I wonder what it would have been like . . .

To kiss him.

I'm grinning ear to ear as the thought rolls around like a persistent marble circling the inside of my skull.

"I like that smile of yours."

I turn around. Russell is standing there. White linen shorts, a Hawaiian shirt all covered in big bright flowers as if he dressed to match the wallpaper. He's taller and thicker than me, and he has a little gut, a belly, which I didn't see in the water, but I find all of him adorable. And that smile. His smile is like sunshine.

"Russell?"

He barks at me. Laughs. Then says, "Rex."

I stand up. "What are you doing here?"

"I'm staying here. What are *you* doing here?"

"This is where I'm staying too."

We both chuckle. Then I remember myself, and crane my neck to look past him, wondering if Jill might be looking for me.

"Worried about your friends?" he asks.

"Sorry," I say.

"Don't apologize," he says. "I remember what it was like."

"What what was like?"

"Not being out."

I look at my book, at my hands gripping the paperback like it might fly away if I don't hold it tight enough.

"It's okay," he says. Then he fishes into his pocket. He takes out a pen, takes my book from me, and writes on a blank page. His full name—Russell Dawes—and his phone number. "You should call me."

"I don't live here. I live in Prattville. Outside Montgomery."

"I don't live here either," Russell says. "I live in New Orleans. Ever visit?"

"No." I look at my book, set in New Orleans. "But I've always wanted to."

He smiles. "You should. Now you have a place to stay."

"Where?" I ask.

He laughs. "With me, stupid."

Then I'm laughing too.

We fall to silence, but our eyes are still locked.

He looks around.

Then he says, "Fuck it." He pushes me into a corner, away from any possible prying eyes, where no one can see, and he kisses me. His lips are softer than velvet. His hand on the small of my back strong, gripping. Then I'm holding his face and kissing him back.

I feel unburdened. Free.

After so many seconds, what seems like a small eternity of hours but in reality is barely a minute, he gently pulls away. Kisses me with a peck. And smirks his little smirk. "I've wanted to do that all day."

"Me too," I whisper.

"Guess you'll have to visit me in New Orleans, then. So we can do it again." As he walks away, he gives a little wave. "You have my number. Use it."

Then he disappears into the elevator. As the doors close, he's still smiling.

My knees are so weak I have to sit down.

I spend the next few days touching my lips. Trying to recapture that moment. And re-create the happiest moment of my life.

barbecue

White smoke rises up from the black metal grill. The curls drift up until they fade, disappearing as they're absorbed into the ether. The sky is blue except for a few tufts of white, like vanilla cotton candy pulled apart. The wind blows across the back of my neck, then stirs the leaves of the tall trees edging the backyard fence. The smell of roasting meat wafts through the air. Dad opens the grill, turns the chicken breasts, then closes the lid.

He's more quiet than usual.

The brown beer bottle goes sideways as he takes another swig. Usually, after two beers, he's all giggles at his own jokes. It's after six or seven beers he gets mean. I don't think he's had that many yet, but already there's a hint of a scowl.

For some reason, he can't look at me.

Which makes no sense. He's the one who called me to come outside. It wasn't a question. He's Air Force. He doesn't ask questions. He gives orders. But it's been minutes, and he hasn't said a word since I asked, "What's up?" and all he said was, "Sit down."

Finally, I speak again. "You okay?"

I don't see it coming. Not from a mile away. His words are like dark night swallowing day. He says, "If you choose to be gay, then you're no longer part of this family."

The air floods out of my lungs. Like he punched me in the chest.

He says, "You want to live that lifestyle? Then do it somewhere else."

All I can manage is, "Wh-what?"

"I know," he says.

"Know what?" I ask. "I haven't done anything."

But that's not true. I think of Russell's kiss. Of my previous crush on Rich, on a dozen men on TV shows and movies. But Dad doesn't know about that. Any of that. I've never said a word. And he can't know my thoughts. If he did, he would have said something a long time ago. Cause these thoughts, these queer fantasies? They've always been there. Since I was little.

Dad downs the rest of the bottle of beer. He puts it down on the table, hard. Not slamming it, but not easing it down either. His hands are shaking. His chin tries to go up, he tries to look at me. He fails.

He turns his back on me, his hands on his hips, his gaze drifting off. Back to the bald cypresses and longleaf pine trees fighting the growing heat of incoming summer. It's not that hot this late in the day, this early in the evening. The sun's up, though not for long. Still, it's only warm, with a cool breeze. Yet I'm boiling inside. Terrified. So much so that sweat soaks through my shirt.

"I don't even know if I am . . ." I begin. But my voice drifts off, disappearing like the smoke from the grill.

I can't defend myself.

Because I don't know.

Am I? Aren't I? Or am I lying to myself? Hiding from the truth.

"I think . . . I just need time to figure it out. I like girls, I do." Which is true. I've had girlfriends. I've never had a boyfriend. But I don't want to lie. "But . . . I think . . . I might . . . I might like guys too."

Somehow, Dad manages to find my face. Without eye contact. His face redder than I've ever seen. His jaw so tight, I expect his teeth to shatter under the pressure.

He growls, "You either are or you aren't."

"But I'm not sure."

It's almost a laugh that leaps out of Dad's throat. Like, "Hah!" But he's doesn't think this is funny. Not in the least.

He asks, "Have you acted on it? These feelings?"

I think of Russell. The touch of our hands in the ocean. The kiss in the hotel.

"Have you?"

I don't want to lie, but the word escapes my mouth before I can stop it. "No."

Dad presses his knuckles to his temples. Starts pacing. This isn't relief. This is anger. He's debating in his head. And I'm hoping his judgment will fall in my favor.

"How . . . how did you know?"

"That isn't the point," he snarls.

I wonder if Dad has always known. Maybe he lied to himself. I couldn't hide it as a boy. I only learned to cover it up as I grew older, trying to become a more masculine version of myself, to protect myself.

Dad finally says, "Rebecca told me."

Rebecca. My stepsister. We're close. So I've dropped hints. I wanted her to know. One time, during a late-night talk, admitting I might be bisexual. I'd hinted at it in high school with a few of my closest friends, but I never said it. And she was my sister. She was safe. She promised she wouldn't say anything to anybody. She promised.

But she told my dad.

Still, somehow I'm not even angry.

Actually, I'm relieved.

It's out. It's in the world. She said it. Made it real. Now Dad knows. Which means my stepmom probably knows. Which means I can't take it back. I don't even know if I want to take it back. Even if the world does hate me. Cause it's been a secret as long as I've been alive, and I hate lying. I hate secrets. I hate keeping this part of me quiet just because it makes someone else uncomfortable. It's not fair.

Dad turns on me, finally looking at my face. "You have a choice. You can stay and be part of this family if—and only if—you abide by the following conditions." He says, "One, you'll see a therapist every week. At your own expense." He says, "Two, you attend church Wednesday night and twice on Sundays—"

"You don't even go to church."

"Don't interrupt me!" he shouts. He takes a breath. He says, "Three, you'll date a girl from church, one that I meet and approve of."

"Are you serious?"

"Goddammit!" he snaps, pointing, like he wants to hit me.

I almost wish he would. That, I'm not afraid of. I've been hit before. Plenty of times. Not by him, but by my mom and stepdad. That's why I came to live here, with my dad, in Alabama. Violence doesn't scare me. But being cast out?

"Four," he continues, "you will never again associate with a person of homosexual persuasion. No friends, no acquaintances, none of that. And five, for all intents and purposes, you will be straight. Is that understood?"

"No," I whisper. "I don't understand."

"You want me to repeat myself?"

I shake my head. "No, I heard you. But it's not that easy," I whisper. "It's not black-and-white for me. Not right now. I don't know who I am yet. I need time to figure it out."

"Well, you need to decide now."

"But I can't."

"Choose," he growls. "Choose right now."

And I can't. I know I can't. Because . . .

"It's not a choice," I say.

"Of course it is," he snaps. "Everything in life is a choice."

The way he looks at me, the disgust in his eyes. I feel five years old again. Not understanding why what I'm feeling is wrong. He stands over me. Like an angry god. Like I'm nothing to him. Less than nothing. Like he stepped in shit, and I'm the bottom of his shoe.

A rush of emotion floods though me. This overwhelming sense of shame. Fear. Helplessness. I've felt it my whole life. And I'm tired of drowning in it. Regret boils up in my throat. The smell of the cooking chicken on the grill makes me gag. I want to throw up.

"You didn't choose to be straight," I realize. "You were born that way. Well, I was born like this."

His fingers curl into fists.

"If you want to stay here, in this house, be a part of this family? You'll do what I say. If not . . ."

The stench of ash fills the air. Something is burning.

Dad turns around, opens the lid, pulls the sizzling pieces of chicken out with tongs, tosses them on a plate, and slams the grill closed. He stares at the meat, the skin etched in black char. "I'm not doing this for me," he says. "I'm doing this for you."

He adds, "If you're gay, you'll ruin your life. You'll never know the joy of getting married, of having a family, of having kids. That's the way things are meant to be. That's the way it's supposed to go. Being gay? It's wrong. It's not natural. People will hate you. You'll get AIDS and die. Alone. Is that what you want?"

A knot forms in my throat, so big I can barely breathe. I've been afraid of AIDS my whole life. And hearing my father say it out loud makes it seem more real. Like he's right. Like maybe I should fold. I should try to be straight. Even if I have to fake it.

"Would you rather be alone, or have a family that loves you?" he asks. "Do you want to be here, with us, or out there, by yourself? Cause that's what you'll be. On your own. By yourself."

It's like I can't see the blue sky. Like every shadow in the back lawn grew, grew so big it consumed the light. Like the whole world's gone dark. Like the future is black. And I can't see anything anymore. Cause all I can see is my fear made real, made solid, into dirt, that's burying me six feet down.

Dad says, "I don't want you to die alone, son. But it's your choice."

I'm shaking.

Cause all I can think is, I've struggled enough. I'm so tired of feeling like this. I can't change. I know that already. My whole life I've tried. Girls are striking, and I want to be with them, but . . . maybe more out of obligation than desire. Cause that's all I've ever seen, in the movies, on TV, in real life. Men and women together. Never a man and a man, or a woman and a woman. Yet no matter how much I've wanted otherwise, I can't help but stare at men. They're so beautiful. Like works of art made flesh. Like they're magnets calling to me.

Nothing is going to change that instinct.

Not even the threat of losing what little family I have left.

"It's not a choice," I say again, trying to push the thought into my dad's mind. To make him understand.

But he won't.

"It is," Dad says, tired. "It's your choice."

As if this conversation never happened, he picks up the plate of overcooked poultry, walks toward the door, and stops, his back to me. He says, "You have twenty-four hours to make up your mind."

Rebecca

When I finally come inside—after I've stopped myself from wanting to puke, after I've kept all the crying inside, not willing to shed a tear, after I've told myself again and again, I am going to figure this out—I see my stepmom wiping her tears in the kitchen. Dad growls, "Set the table so we can eat already." She glances up, her eyes apologetic. Then she does what Dad says.

I walk to my room. On the way is Rebecca's. My stepsister, fifteen, sitting on the floor, holding a stuffed pink bear, like she did when she was little, when she was upset. She's rocking back and forth. She's crying too. "I'm sorry," she says, "I didn't think he would—"

"It's okay," I say.

"No, it's not," she says, breaking into little sobs. "Why is he being like this? Why is he doing this? Who cares if you're—"

"He does."

"I don't care," she says. Looking up, wells of tears in her

eyes, she says, "You know that, right? I love you no matter what. You'll always be my brother."

"I know." Then I'm hugging her, and she's crying harder. And it takes every effort for me not to fall apart with her.

"I'm so sorry," she sobs. "I'm so, so, so sorry. I thought if I told him, maybe he'd be okay. Maybe he'd be all right with it. That it would all be fine. I didn't know he was going to freak out. I didn't know—"

My neck is wet from all her tears.

"I hate him. Fucking asshole."

"It's okay," I say, not sure if I believe it. "It's gonna be okay."

"No, it's not! He's kicking you out, Rex!"

As she sobs, an ache in my body turns to actual physical pain in my stomach. An excruciating stabbing. It tries to grow, but I push it down. And I squeeze my hands to stop them from shaking.

"Come on. Don't worry about me. I've been through worse," I say. "I'm like a cat. I always land on my feet."

"But you don't have nine lives," Rebecca says. "You just have the one."

numbers

It's been twenty-three hours. I owe Dad a decision. Except I've already made up my mind, and if I say it out loud, I know I can't stay. Still, part of me hopes he'll change his mind. Maybe he'll come around. Maybe he'll realize all of this is okay, that I'm not some kind of abomination. Maybe at the last possible minute, he'll fold.

See that he's wrong.

Right?

I'm sitting on the edge of the bed, looking around the room. The white shutters on the windows. The white walls with tall ceilings. The queen-sized mattress. The antique armoire. None of this is mine. It belongs to my dad. It's a guest room he donated to me when I needed a safe haven to restart my life.

I came here, to Alabama, to live with my dad. It was supposed to be my fresh start. No more fighting, no more violence from my mom and stepdad. I knew it wouldn't be perfect, but I didn't think this was where we'd end up.

I flip through my notebook, the one with all my phone numbers. It only has a few numbers of people here in Alabama. Most are friends from work, from Walmart. All of them are people who don't know about me. People who wouldn't be okay with it. People who can't help me.

Some of the numbers are for my old friends in Texas. Some who I've chatted with since I moved. Most who I haven't stayed in touch with. Not cause I didn't want to, but cause I was busy working full-time, trying to get ready for college. I regret not calling them now.

The rest of the numbers are family.

Like my mom and stepdad. Who are crazy. Who used to beat me. Who I refuse to call for help.

Then my abuela. My mom's mom. My only living grandparent. She's always been there for me. But this? This might be too much. She's Church of Christ. Super-religious, with a belief system that doesn't agree with me. When I was growing up, she took me to churches that preached homosexuality was a sin. I don't know what I would say to her now. Why my dad is kicking me out. Why I need to return to Abilene, Texas.

But what if she rejected me? What if she turned her back on me too? I don't think I could take it. Not from her. It's better for me not to know. For her not to know.

And I don't want to return to Abilene. I don't want to go backward. I need to move forward. Everything is going to be okay. I just have to figure this out.

So why am I on the verge of tears?

Pulling a duffel bag out of the closet, I start packing it with as much as can fit. Shirts, shorts, socks, underwear. I fight back a rush of emotions. My stomach churns.

Where am I going to go?

On the floor, next to my backpack, is the copy of *Interview with the Vampire*. Set in New Orleans. Where I know a man with a smile that stops my heart.

extension

Twenty-four hours are up. My cheeks are stained with tears. I wipe them. I don't want to seem weak. I'm trying to get my feet to move, to carry me to the front door. But they can't.

Dad shows up in the doorway. He asks, "What's your decision?"

"I don't want to go," I say.

"That's not what I asked."

"I'm thinking!" I shout.

He hesitates.

He turns to walk away, hesitates, and says, "Think hard, then. You have 'til morning to decide."

good-bye

The sun rises.

Tears streaming down her face, Mona, my stepmom, pulls at my dad's arm. "Don't do this. He's your only son."

His arms are crossed across his chest as he stands in the hallway. He asks me, "Why are you still here?"

"Are you really going to do this?" I ask, trying not to choke on the knot in my throat.

"I told you, the choice is yours."

"Quit using that as a defense. You're kicking me out."

"If that's what you want to believe, I can't stop you."

Her door wide open, Rebecca is sitting on her bedroom floor again. Crying out, "You can't, Dad. You can't."

Looking at me, Dad points toward the front door. "Your time is up."

My eyes burn. I take deep, heavy breaths that make me dizzy. Mona is sobbing now. Repeating to her husband, "Don't do this."

I pick up my backpack, slip into its grip, and turn to my father. I keep waiting for him to change his mind. To say he was wrong. To apologize. To say I can stay.

But his lips are pressed together in a fine line of determination. If he feels any remorse, he's not showing it.

I pick up my duffel bag, throwing the strap over my shoulder.

And I walk toward the front door.

———

Outside, on the front porch, my dad stands there like a golem made of stone. He's hard. Unmoving. He's made up his mind. And he's not changing it.

Mona and Rebecca hug me from either side. Rebecca has finally stopped crying, but she can't stop sniffling. Mona's face is wet with tears too. She pulls my chin up and looks me in the eyes. "I love you, you know that? I will always love you."

"Don't go," Rebecca says. "He can't make you leave."

"Yes, he can," I say.

"What's he going to do?"

I look at him, at his cold blue eyes. He's angry. He's upset. He thinks I made the wrong choice—as if it were a choice at all. But I know his ferocity. I saw it in my mom. In my stepdad. Just before they raised their fists. My dad is willing to get violent if he needs to. He'll shove me out of the house if I try to go back in.

I can't choose to stay, but I can choose how I leave.

I refuse to make a big scene.

I won't be pushed out.

This is my choice.

I choose this.

I hug my stepsister and stepmom one more time. Then I

walk in front of my dad. His face is frigid, his eyes dark despite the blue. His face isn't calculating. He's made up his mind. He won't budge. Not on this.

I step off the porch, and walk forward. I throw my stuff into the passenger side of my green pickup truck. I shut the door gently. Walking around the front of my truck, I get in. I sit there for a long time, staring.

The green, mowed lawn. The manicured shrubs. The family on the porch. The picture-perfect home. The only thing wrong with the image are the faces. No one is happy.

Rebecca storms past my dad into the house, shouting something as she passes. Mona stands on the porch, distraught. Then follows her daughter inside.

I insert the key into the ignition and press down on the clutch. I turn the key, and the engine roars to life.

I take my time. Waiting for my dad to step forward. To cry out for me to stop. Even now. Any minute he might reconsider. I pause, like an inmate on death row, hoping for the phone to ring. A last-minute save.

But with every second, hope crumbles inside me. Piece by piece breaking away, igniting into flame, until there's nothing left. Nothing but ashes.

He stands there. Arms crossed. Certain.

Finally, I stop waiting.

I put the truck in reverse. Pull out of the driveway onto the road. Wrestle the stick shift into first. Then I press the gas.

And just like that, I'm homeless.

then

Driving.

Hot tears down my cheeks.

I want to hit myself. I should have known this was coming.

Thinking back to when I was five. In kindergarten. All of us children sitting on the colorful carpet, made dim as the lights turned off and the movie projector was turned on. Cartoon animals danced across the screen, and the class laughed and giggled.

At the front of the room, I noticed Claire and Lisa holding hands. They were always holding hands. They were best friends.

Mikey was my best friend. So I reached my hand over and placed it on his. He looked at it for only a second, then squeezed. On-screen, the boy rabbit and the girl duck kissed. So I kissed Mikey.

That's when Ms. Forester grabbed me by the arm, and yanked me up. She dragged me to the front office, her grip so tight my arm burned. She told Principal Johnson what had happened. He looked at me from across his desk and said only the one word, "Disgusting." He called my father.

When Dad showed up at my school, his face was the color of a fire truck and he was gnashing his teeth. He apologized to the principal, said he'd handle it. He didn't speak to me the whole ride to his place. When we got into his apartment, he took off his belt.

What happened next didn't work. All it did was make me hide.

I spent the next thirteen years hiding.

Until now.

Now, driving into the unknown, I can't hide anymore.

what I have

The radio plays on my truck radio, but I can't hear the songs. I'm too busy trying to breathe. Trying to think. What am I doing? I'm going to New Orleans . . . but where am I going to live? I'll find somewhere . . . but how am I going to eat? I'll get a job . . . but when is this feeling of danger going to go away? Or will it never go away?

Deep breaths.

I try to think of what I have.

My truck.

A full tank of gas.

The clothes on my body:

Underwear, socks, jean shorts, a T-shirt, a ball cap, shoes.

My backpack, which contains:

A toothbrush. Toothpaste. Deodorant. A few paperback books.

My duffel bag, which contains:

Underwear, socks, shorts, a pair of jeans, shirts, a sweatshirt, a hoodie.

My wallet, which contains:

My Social Security card, my driver's license, a video rental card, the book page scribbled with Russell's phone number, and one hundred and seventeen dollars.

There's also some change in my pocket.

I never thought I would have so little. Not when I need so much.

miles between

Three hundred and twenty-three miles stretch out between Prattville, Alabama, and New Orleans, Louisiana. South and west on Interstate 65 and on to Interstate 10.

Driving through Montgomery to Hope Hull to Letohatchee, then passing Fort Deposit, Greenville, Bolling, Georgiana, Evergreen, Atmore . . .

On either side of the road are towering trees with thick-barked columns, branches bristling with green, several stories tall. The way the wind pushes them, the way the sky is blue, the way others are driving along, not a care in the world, I realize that my dad was right about one thing. I'm alone. And no one knows any better.

One thing I've never noticed about Alabama is how beautiful it is. Not just the trees, but the grass, the hills, the bodies of water. I didn't appreciate it. It's a state of segregation and homophobia. But now that it isn't going to be my home any longer? Now I almost miss it. But I keep driving.

As I skirt the city of Mobile, I notice a sign for Pensacola. And I think of Russell. He's one of the reasons I'm going to New Orleans. Maybe the top reason.

But I'm also going because I've always wanted to go. Ever since I started reading Anne Rice. Her romantic view of the city makes it seem like a dark and magical place. And it can't be a coincidence that Russell lives there. It's as if the universe is trying to tell me something.

In stories since the dawn of time, the hero leaves home to search out his great love. Isn't that what I'm doing? Like the mermaid Ariel, I'm going to a whole new world for someone I barely know. It could be the best thing I've ever done.

Or it could be a huge mistake.

I try to push that thought from my head. Focus on the positive. Everything is going to work out for the best. It has to.

I'm driving through the foot of Mississippi. And what's the rush? I pull back my foot from the gas pedal, slowing down to below the speed limit on the 90 so I can drift along the side of the beach and spy on the ocean. Salty air flushes in through my rolled-down window. I move through Biloxi. Gulfport. Long Beach. Then, Pass Christian, a town name that sounds like "past Christian," making me laugh, though I'm not sure why. Over the Bay St. Louis Bridge, and on for a bit until I'm back on I-10 in the homestretch to my destination. Past Slidell and Eden Isle, and then across the Twin Span Bridge, two lines of road stretched across the water like concrete snakes.

The air is already hot, but now it thickens, humidity washing over me like a warm blanket in the summer, as I approach my future on the horizon.

I don't know where to go, so I choose signs that feel right until I find myself in the famous French Quarter. The buildings are just like Anne Rice described them—a mix of French, Spanish, and Caribbean styles forming something new. I think she called it the Creole style, but I can't remember now. And I don't care. I've never seen any place like it. Pastel homes and businesses have window shutters, cast-iron balconies, and rectangular columns. Some of the roads are paved with stones instead of asphalt. I think of the Vampire Lestat, and wonder if there's any chance vampires are real, and I might be turned into one and live forever.

In the distance, I hear jazz music and the dim roar of a crowd. It takes a long while to find a spot, but I finally park my truck, get out, and walk toward the sounds. I find myself on Bourbon Street, parades of people pouring into and out of roaring bars, wearing shiny plastic beads, drinking from three-foot-tall plastic cups in neon colors. I walk past Cajun restaurants with fresh jambalaya and coffeehouses with signs for beignets.

I have no idea what a beignet is, but people are swarming in droves to get them. So I follow, entering some place called Café du Monde, intoxicated by the smell. Hunger overtakes me, so I buy half a dozen. The square-shaped dough is deep-fried golden brown, dusted with confectioner's sugar, and melts in my mouth.

I've never tasted anything so good.

Everywhere here there is life, bustling about, music throbbing like a heartbeat, like this is the center of the universe.

A smile wraps around me. Calm comes over me. So many people. So many places. So much opportunity. Maybe . . . maybe things will work out.

quarter

It's late afternoon when I realize I should have already made the call. My fingers jingle the change in my jean shorts pocket. I pull them out, carefully sorting through the coins, careful not to drop a single penny, until I find a quarter. At a pay phone, I get out my wallet and retrieve the page with Russell's number on it. I take a moment to admire the soft curves of his handwriting in blue ink. It makes me smile, thinking of that night in the hotel lobby and the reunion that is about to take place.

I roll the quarter into the slot, *ka-chink*, then wait for the ringtone. Punching the small silver buttons, I dial the number.

It rings.

It rings again.

And suddenly I'm worried he's not home. Or, worse, that this isn't really his number. What if he made a mistake when he wrote it down? What if—

"Hello?"

A wave of relief washes over me.

"Russell. It's Rex."

"Rex?" He hesitates. Then he barks. I can't help but laugh. "How's it going, little buddy?"

"You'll never guess where I am."

"No way. Are you here?" he asks, his southern drawl making me swoon a little. "In New Orleans?"

"I am. Can we meet up tonight?"

"Oh man. I'm sorry, but I have plans."

My heart drops.

He asks, "Why didn't you give me a heads-up a few days ago?"

"It was kind of a last-minute trip."

"Well, you're here now. Look, I can't reschedule tonight. I'm on my way out the door. But let's grab dinner tomorrow night if you're free."

Suddenly it dawns on me. I didn't think this through. Where am I going to sleep tonight? I hadn't assumed it would be at Russell's, but I hadn't considered where else it would be either. I don't know anybody else in New Orleans. And I can't afford a hotel.

"Hello? You there?" Russell asks.

"Yeah. Tomorrow night sounds great."

"Can't wait to kiss your face."

My heart finds a buoy at the thought of Russell's lips.

I say, "Same."

"Call me tomorrow at six. I'll think of somewhere nice to take you."

"Sounds great."

"See you tomorrow."

When I hang up the phone, I look around. The buzz of

people washes over me. This isn't the worst place to be alone. How can you be alone, surrounded by people?

But as I walk around, the sun begins to set and the shadows grow long. Somehow the oncoming darkness seems overwhelming. Impenetrable. Like the absence of light is going to press down until it crushes me under its weight.

———

I wander the streets on foot. Wandering up and down Bourbon Street. Watching people go about their lives.

Folks of all shapes and sizes laugh among their groups of friends. Some gaze about at their surroundings, taking in the tourist sights, snapping photos with cameras. Some are slow-footed, drunk, trying to walk, or slumped against walls. From a balcony, a man yells down to a group of women, "Show us your tits." One of them considers, her girlfriends egging her on. Finally, she lifts her shirt, as fast as she can, exposing her lacy bra, and pulls it down again. The man on the balcony throws down a necklace of gold plastic beads. She catches them and places them around her neck, cheered by her friends.

The lights, the music, they feel alive. When I was growing up in Texas, everything felt so buttoned-up. In Alabama, everyone felt so stifled. Here, there is a freedom. Like anything goes.

It makes me think of the word *bacchanalia*. My brain takes a minute to remember it's derived from Bacchus, the Roman god of pleasure, who was based on the Greek deity Dionysus, god of wine and ecstasy. I did a book report in high school and debated including the mention of orgies. I added it, and the teacher drew a red line through that passage in permanent marker, as if banishing it. But there is no banishment here.

There's an energy to this city like I've never felt.

"Watch it," a straggler snaps as he stumbles out of a bar and slams into me. He takes two more steps, then pukes on the stone-cobbled street. He wipes his mouth, then saunters back inside.

Despite what I just saw, my stomach churns. I realize I'm thirsty. It was a hot day, I need water. And I need dinner.

I open my wallet and count my money. It won't last long. I have to be careful about how I spend each and every dollar. There's no paycheck coming in to rescue me.

Suddenly I remember my job at Walmart. I should be working right now.

I never even called in to quit. After all, some part of me thought my dad would cave. He'd change his mind and let me stay. It never seemed real. Even now, it doesn't. It feels like I'm on vacation. Like I can go back.

But I can't.

I wonder if Jill and Rich are wondering where I am, since I won't show tonight. Or tomorrow. By the end of the week, they'll consider what happened. They'll call my house, and my dad or Rebecca or Mona will have to explain. What are they going to say?

A pit opens in my stomach. I realize I don't want Jill to know I'm gay. Or Rich. Cause he'll question my motives in our friendship, question whether I ever checked him out. Cause I know Jill will think it's a sin. She'll pray for me. And I don't want her prayers. I just want her to accept me for me, and still want to be my friend.

But already, I know. I'll never go back to Alabama.

That chapter of my life is done.

————

My stomach growls.

So I find a Popeyes, and get the cheapest meal they have. A child's size chicken tender basket with fries. It comes with a small Coke. The dinner doesn't fill me up, so I take advantage of the free refills on soda until I'm over-amped from the sugar and caffeine.

Having no idea what time it is, I'm wide awake. I should have brought my book. I could read at the table, keep getting refills. But already they're beginning to mop. "We're closing," the woman says. I go to the bathroom one last time. Washing my hands, I take a long look in the mirror. I still look like me.

"It's going to be fine," I whisper to myself. "Everything is going to work out."

I wander to Jackson Square, where I find a bench. I sit for a long time. A few tourists mill about. A few homeless people walk past like zombies. One is muttering to himself. Another screams at a tree.

"I'm going to be okay," I say. Though I don't know how convincing my own voice is. Not when it cracks halfway through.

Eventually I make my way back to my truck. Away from the crowds, the night seems more oppressive. Not just the humidity, but the darkness itself. Only the streetlights break it up, each spaced at a small distance from the next.

Once in my truck, I lock the doors. I tuck my duffel bag into the passenger foot space, and use my backpack as a pillow. I wiggle around on the bucket seats, curling into a fetal position as if I could shrink myself. But the truck's cab seems somehow smaller than it ever has before and I can't get comfortable. It doesn't help that the belt buckle stabs me in the spine if I move even an inch.

I don't sleep well. Probably hyped up from the caffeine, my mind wanders between waking and dreaming.

I dream memories from when I was little. From when I was seven, obsessed with Spider-Man. Pretending I could shoot webs from my wrists and swing between buildings by jumping from couch to chair and back again. From when my school took our class to see a ballet called *Swan Lake*. The dancers were beautiful and elegant in their movement. Perfect control of arms and legs, graceful. When I got home, dancing replaced my web-slinging. Until I told my stepdad I wanted to be a ballerina, and he told me to stop acting like a sissy.

Then the world contracts, closing in on me. And I'm five again, back with my dad, who is standing over me, belt in hand, fury etched across his face. Only this time I grow smaller, dwindling, shame shrinking my tiny frame more and more. I am the size of a melon, and then a cockroach, and then a piece of dust. And, eventually, I just cease to exist.

Only, my thoughts are still there, trapped in the dark eternity of oblivion. But I'm alone.

As I slowly wake, caught between consciousness and unconsciousness, all I can think is, I should have been born normal. I should have been stronger. I should have willed myself to behave like normal men, to love women, like god wants, like my dad wants. I should have made the right decision. Instead, I chose wrong. And now? Now I deserve whatever comes next.

remnants

Walking Bourbon Street during the early morning doesn't have the same magic as the night before. The cobble-stoned streets are littered with crushed plastic cups and broken bead necklaces, leftovers of the party that went on until the late hours. A footprint smears a flyer for a jazz band next to a rat lying dead on the bricked sidewalk. The stench of spilled alcohol is so intense, it makes my eyes burn. Loud trucks arrive, both to clean the streets and deliver men pushing new kegs into the bars for tonight. The Bacchus-fueled revelry is gone, replaced by families, stopping to take pictures in front of the weatherworn buildings.

With the sun beating down, any vampires are asleep, and I'm disappointed I didn't meet one.

It's hotter than last night, and the humidity is overwhelming. Streams of sweat pour down my skin between T-shirt and backpack. I need to find shade for the next few hours, or I'll sweat out every drop of water in my system.

I find a store with a blasting air conditioner. I pretend to admire the merchandise: guide maps, shot glasses, shirts, stuffed animals, magnets, snow globes, walls of plastic beads in every metallic color you can imagine. I stay until I'm shivering. Then, without buying anything, I walk outside, back into the sweltering heat.

I wander in and out of shops and art galleries, pretending that I belong. That I'm another tourist. Missing are my sunglasses, my visor, my newly purchased T-shirt with NEW ORLEANS printed across it in various fonts. Missing is the camera around my neck, ready to snap a picture of historical buildings or a funeral procession. Missing is my family.

So many of the daytime tourists walk around in units of three or four or five or more. The curious child, the annoyed teenager, the excited mom, the frustrated dad, sometimes an aunt or uncle or grandparent. I ignore the pang in my heart. I am alone, but I am free. I don't have to take orders from anyone. I can be myself.

But how much is it costing me?

I look at my watch. Still hours to go before I can call Russell.

first date

Over the phone, Russell gives me directions to his place. On the way, I get lost twice. By the time I arrive, it's dark.

I drive up Pantheon Avenue, counting the numbers on houses and mailboxes until I find it. Parking on the street, I shove my duffel bag and backpack behind the truck seats so no one will see a reason to break in.

The front steps lead up to a gabled front porch. The house is slim, but long, has a gingerbread trim, but it's painted all in white. My heart beats harder in my chest, my nerves frayed. What if he doesn't like me? What if he made a mistake? What if tonight goes badly?

I force myself to knock on the door. By the time he answers, I feel sick to my stomach.

He's in a towel, standing there dripping wet, the smile I remember splashed across his face. I look at the doorframe, trying not to be turned on—and failing. "Don't be shy. Come on in," he says. "I need to finish getting ready."

He disappears into the bathroom, as I stand awkwardly in the living room. There's a futon couch, a TV on a stand, a potted plant. An air conditioner hangs out of the window, blasting a small stream of cool air inside. Adjacent is a kitchen, with a humming fridge, a sink, a small table in the center of the room. No dishwasher. Curious, I look through the sliding doors into the bedroom, where there's a large bed, a dresser, and a framed poster of a country singer on the wall. Beyond that is a small hallway that leads to the bathroom and a back room filled with boxes and clothes. From the wooden floors and the exposed brick, I can tell this is an older house. But it has all kinds of charm. Like Russell.

On a side table there's a picture of Russell smiling with his family. I wonder if they know about him being gay.

"Okay, all good to go," he says, coming up from behind me. He wears a polo shirt, khaki shorts, and a spray of cologne. "You ready for our first date?"

I nod. Nerves are vibrating my insides. I don't know what to expect.

Russell grabs his keys from the counter, and a bottle of wine. "Hold this," he says, walking me outside, locking the door, then directing me to the Jeep in his driveway. "You like Cajun food?"

"I don't know. I've never had it."

"Hot dog! You are in for a treat."

Russell watches the road, but he keeps stealing glances at me. "What?" he asks. I realize I've been staring at him.

"Nothing," I say. "You're just cuter than I remember."

"So are you."

He reaches over and takes my hand in his.

We park on a neighborhood street, walking down the block to a small restaurant with a patio dining area. Smooth and soulful jazz music flutters down lightly from a speaker overhead. A waitress says, "Sit anywhere."

Russell directs me to a table with a red-and-white-checkered plastic tablecloth. He shuffles through the caddy holding napkins, hot sauce, utensils. He finds a bottle opener. He cuts the foil seal off the top of the wine bottle, and twists the corkscrew into the cork. When he pulls it, there's a slight *plop*. "I like this place. Food's good and cheap. And it's BYOB."

"BYOB?"

"Bring your own beer. Or in this case, wine. Cause I'm classy like that."

Without a word, the waitress drops off two empty cups and two menus. Then steers toward another table of customers.

Russell pours me a glass of wine, and then one for himself.

My eyes widen. I watch the waitress disappear into the kitchen, then whisper to Russell, "I'm not twenty-one. I can't drink. I'll get in trouble."

Russell chortles. "No one cares. Welcome to the city that care forgot." Russell raises his glass, and I do the same. "Cheers."

I take a sip of the room-temperature red wine, letting it slide down my throat. I drank beer and liquor in high school, but I've never had wine before. I like it.

"You are eighteen, right?" Russell asks.

I realize my being seventeen could be a problem. So I nod. I tell myself it's not a lie if I'm simply nodding. But Russell seems to hesitate. It just rolls off my tongue, "Yeah. Eighteen."

"Whew," Russell says.

"How old are you?"

"Thirty-one."

I do the math in my head. He was in middle school when

I was being born. Somehow, it doesn't bother me. I kind of like that he's older. More mature. I take another sip of wine.

Russell does the same. He says, "I'm glad you called. I'm glad you're here."

"Me too."

"So what brings you to town?"

I swallow hard. What do I tell him? I can't tell him what happened—can I? What would he say? Would he be freaked out? Wonder what I want from him? Would he think less of me? Would he end the date? Would he be done with me?

I say, "I just drove down here."

"By yourself?"

"By myself."

"For no reason?"

"I've never been here before. And I've been reading all about it in *Interview with the Vampire*. You know, that Anne Rice book. So, yeah. I wanted to see New Orleans."

"N'awlins."

"Huh?"

"Locals pronounce it N'awlins."

"N'awlins."

"Atta boy," he says. He takes another sip of wine. He slurps it, so the sound ripples at the edge of his lips. "So what do you think?"

"Of what?"

"Of whatever. What's on your mind?"

I shrug.

"You seem distracted."

"No. I'm not," I say, grabbing a breath. "I'm just . . . I guess . . . Sorry, I know it's stupid, but I'm nervous."

"Nervous? Why?"

I lean in to whisper, "I've never been on a date with a . . . a guy before."

Russell beams. "I'm your first?"

"You are."

"I'm honored." He bows his head slightly, coming up with a grin. "If it makes you feel any better, I'm nervous too."

"You are?"

"Yeah. I've never been on a date with someone so cute."

I feel my cheeks flush.

"It's all good," Russell says, taking my hand under the table. Then he leans in too, whispering, "Sorry, we gotta hold hands under the table, but as progressive as this city is, we're still in the South."

"That's okay," I say. His hand is warm, comforting. Somehow I feel more relaxed knowing he's nervous too.

"If you ever need to wash your clothes, there's a laundromat next door to here. Works out well. You come, put a load in the wash, then have dinner and chill out 'til it's time to put your clothes in the dryer. Then you come back and have dessert and another drink."

"Oh, cool."

"Guess that doesn't matter to you, since you don't live here."

"Right," I say. After another drink of wine, I add, "But I'm thinking about it. Moving here, I mean."

"No shit?"

"Yeah, I just . . . it's time for a change. And Alabama's not for me."

"And you're really thinking about moving?"

"Sure. I mean, there's colleges in the city, right?"

"There's Tulane, Loyola, Xavier, University of N'awlins," Russell says. "Are you for real about going to school here?"

"Why not?"

"No, I'd be happy if you did. We could be boyfriends."

My heart skips a beat.

"You okay dating an older man?" he asks.

"You're not that old."

"When I was graduating high school, you were in diapers."

"No, I wasn't!"

Russell tries to talk me into the red beans and rice or the gumbo, but I don't like beans and the last thing I want is hot soup. Russell goes with the crawfish étouffée, and I order the jambalaya. As soon as the waitress leaves, I realize I'm spending money again. But I justify it, reminding myself I haven't eaten all day.

Which is probably why I'm already getting tipsy and laughing at every little thing that comes out of Russell's mouth. He's laughing back. Every once in a while, when there's a lull in the conversation, he barks at me—which just makes me giggle more.

"You're really too cute," he says again. "And butch."

"Me?"

"Yeah, you. When I first saw you, I didn't know if you were or you weren't. Gay, I mean. But there was something about you . . . you were all tough and stuff. Like a real man."

"I wasn't always. Guess I was kind of effeminate when I was little. Other kids figured it out before I did. They called me girlie, stuff like that. But it didn't seem like a big deal. Not until fourth grade when my family moved to a new town and I had to start over at a new school. All these kids I didn't know started calling me names on the playground—gaywad and homo and faggot. I didn't even know what any of those meant. So when I got home, I asked my mom. She said, 'Men who have sex with men. Women who have sex with women. People who have AIDS.'

"I didn't know much about AIDS, but I thought it only killed gay people. That there wasn't a cure. And I was terrified of dying.

"So I knew, I didn't want anything to do with being gay.

"I watched the other guys I went to school with. It was Texas, so there were lots of cowboys and football players. All these jocks, right? They had deep voices and wore baseball caps and walked all tough, chins up, eyes that didn't turn away from anything or anyone. They had all this confidence. I wasn't like that at all. So I studied them. I tried to copy the way they walked, the way they talked, the way they flirted with girls. I had to. I had to become them in order to survive them.

"I even dated a bunch of girls. But I always had crushes on guys. So I tried to push that part of me down. I didn't want to be gay. I didn't want to die of AIDS."

This silence stretches out between us.

Then Russell says, "Damn, kid. Way to bring down the mood."

"Shit. I'm sorry. That was so stupid of me to bring it up."

"Hey, it's cool. I was just kidding," Russell says. "You were being real. I like that. So many gay dudes just talk about clothes and hair and sex and stupid stuff like that. But you're really deep. Mature, even. Guess you have an old soul."

Then he says, "You know you don't just catch a disease from being gay, right?"

"Yeah. I mean, I know that now. But it still scares me."

"I get that. Trust me. I really do. I'm scared of HIV and AIDS too. But that's why they invented condoms."

"True." Only, when I speak, I notice my voice slurs. Russell catches it too. "I think that glass of wine went straight to my head."

"You're a lightweight," Russell says. "One glass of wine and you're drunk."

"I'm not drunk."

"Yeah, you are. You lush." Russell gives me a wink, then refills the wine in my glass.

The waitress appears with our food. I inhale the aroma of my dish. It's made of rice, a mix of chicken, shrimp, and sausage, along with diced peppers, onions, and spices I can't name. But after I take my first bite, I can't stop myself. I'm devouring bite after bite.

Russell raises an eyebrow. "Hungry boy."

"Growing boy," I say, mouth full.

"I bet you are," Russell says with a mischievous grin. He rubs my leg under the table. I almost choke on a slice of sausage.

"So what do you do? You in college?" he asks.

I recall I'm supposed to start in the fall. But that's not happening now. Now that I've left. Still, I say, "Yup, Auburn. But like I said, I'm thinking of transferring. I'm going to stay with some friends until I figure it out."

"You have friends down here? Anyone I know?"

The lies keep flowing out like the wine going down my throat. I shake my head. "I doubt it. They're straight." I swallow another bite of jambalaya, then change the subject. "What do you do? For work, I mean?"

"I work for UPS. You know those brown uniforms? That's

me." He takes another bite of his dinner, chews, swallows, continues. "I skipped college, went straight into the army after high school. I served for eight years, then left to start a life here. I wasn't out in the military, and it started to become an issue. For me, I mean. It's hard being on a boat with a lot of other men day in and day out. Lots of crushes that you can't do anything about."

"I can imagine."

"You really can't." Russell snickers. "Still, I love the army. So I'm in the reserves. That means, if there's a national emergency, I get called in."

"Do you wear one of those cute little white hats?" I ask.

"I sure do. Want me to put it on later?"

I blush again, for probably the twentieth time this evening.

By the time I finish my second glass of wine, I feel like I'm floating. When I blink, my eyelids stay closed half a second too long. But Russell is adorable, so when he refills my glass with the last of the wine, I don't object.

We talk for another hour, about movies (we both like rom-coms), music (he loves country music, I love pop and alternative), stuff we like (we both love the beach). It feels like we have almost everything in common. Like I made the right move coming here. When he picks up the tab for dinner, a sense of relief washes over me. Not just cause I don't have to pay for the meal, but cause he's chivalrous. He's kind. He's everything a guy could want in another guy.

"Thank you for dinner. For paying, I mean," I say. As we stand up, my head starts spinning. I had too much to drink.

"My pleasure. You can take me out next time."

It feels like the floor falls out below me, and I stumble.

"Whoa, easy, there," Russell says, catching me. "You really are a lightweight."

"Is he okay?" the waitress asks.

"He's a tourist," Russell says, as if that explains it. He helps me outside, and we turn the corner and walk toward his Jeep.

But my thoughts start spinning. I can't afford dinner for two. I'm lying to my new boyfriend. Not that he's my boyfriend. Even if I want him to be. Maybe he will be, though. So how can I start off our relationship by lying? That'd be wrong. If he ever found out, he'd never trust me again. He'd think I was a liar. That I was trying to trick him. And he'd be right.

And I like him so much. But I already lied. How can I change my story now? Why didn't I just tell him the truth?

Cause I was worried. That he would reject me. That I'd be alone. Just like Dad said I would be. Now I start thinking about dying alone, of AIDS, of burning in hell. About how I have no one to turn to. My dad done with me. My abuela too religious to understand. And my mom, I don't want to go back there ever. Especially not begging for a place to stay.

I don't have anywhere else to go.

I take a breath. And another one. Trying to calm my racing heart.

I don't need to deal with this. Not right now. Not when I'm drunk. Tomorrow I can figure everything out. One step at a time.

I crawl up into Russell's Jeep. I buckle my seat belt as he puts the keys in the ignition. He turns up the music. I roll down the window, letting the warm night air wash over me.

When we get back to his place, I hop down, and stagger. Russell laughs. "You can't drive home. Not like that."

"*Pfff*," I say. "I'll just sleep in my truck."

"Or you could come in and watch a movie until you sober up."

"What movie?"

"I have *Clueless* on DVD."

"I love that movie."

"Done and done," Russell says, swinging his set of keys around his finger. He unlocks the door and holds it for me to walk in first.

Inside, the air is just as stifling as it is outside. But when Russell turns on the air conditioner, a river of brisk air flows into the house, and I stand in front of it, rubbing my hands in front of it like it's a fire. It's sobering, but not enough. "Make yourself at home," he says, and the word *home* sticks in my ear.

He pours me a glass of water and hands it to me. After he puts the DVD in the player, he sits on the futon couch and pats the seat next to him. "Don't be shy. I won't bite." He smirks. "Unless you want me to."

I sit next to him, and he presses play on the remote. The movie starts, and by the time Cher and Dionne are on their way to school, I find myself relaxing. The swimming in my head lessens—though it doesn't go away. Not completely.

I can't believe so little wine got me drunk. I'm embarrassed, realizing how immature I probably seem, like the teenager I am. Then Russell puts his arm around me. I can't help but snuggle up close. His body feels so familiar, so right. Like I've been missing this my whole life. A new kind of comfort that's so perfect in every way.

And before I know it . . .

I'm asleep.

————

When I wake up halfway through the night, I find myself on Russell's futon. A blanket is draped over me. His snoring sounds in the next room. I think, Even his snoring is comforting. As I drift off again, I find myself smiling.

————

"Want some cereal?" Russell asks.

I rub my fists into my eyes, open them. Russell is standing there in his brown uniform. "Oh no. I can't believe I fell asleep."

Russell laughs it off. "And we didn't even get a chance to make out."

"I'm so sorry," I say, sitting up. "I don't know what came over me."

"Uh, that would be the bottle of wine I fed you. My bad," he says. "Breakfast?" He waves to a box of Cheerios and two bowls in the kitchen. I get up as he pours the cereal and milk and hands me a spoon. We can't stop glancing at each other as we eat.

I ask, "What?"

"What?" he repeats.

We laugh.

"What are your friends going to think?"

"Friends?" I ask.

"Who you're staying with," he says. "You were out all night. Are they going to be worried?"

"Oh. No, no, it's fine. I'll just tell them . . ."

"You spent the night with the most handsome gentleman you've ever met?" Russell smiles. "You can also call me Prince Charming."

I can't help but grin back.

"That's exactly what I'll tell them," I lie. "I really am sorry I fell asleep. I hope I didn't ruin the date."

"Nah. The date was fantastic," he says. "Confession? I'm glad you passed out. If you hadn't, I would have tried to seduce you. And it's better if we wait."

"Yeah?"

"I really like you, kiddo."

"I really like you too."

"Can I see you again?"

"Absolutely."

"Tonight?"

"Tonight."

"You have a number I can call?"

Hesitating, I try to think of an excuse. "Yeah, I mean, no. I don't want to give out my friends' number. But I promise to call tonight. Just tell me what time."

"I'll be home from work by six."

"I'll call you then."

We finish our cereal, and Russell puts on his shoes. He walks me outside, locks his door, and turns around, facing me. He puts his hand under my chin, and kisses me. It's long, and slow. Perfect.

"Tonight, then?" he whispers.

"Tonight."

wander

I'm back in the French Quarter. Cause being around the tourists makes me feel like a tourist. Like I'm just visiting this part of my life where I've been cast out, my family is gone, and I'm on my own for the first time.

I stroll in and out of art galleries. I admire oil paintings showing the streets of New Orleans. Sculptures of all sizes and materials. Splashes of vibrant colors on canvases. Black-and-white photographs of oceans and cliffsides.

Every time I walk out, I am blasted with a powerful heat and humidity. But each time I open a gallery door and step inside, I am greeted with a torrent of cold air, pure relief from the outdoor onslaught.

Someone bangs at the gallery's front window, making me jump. A burly man with a frizzy, unkempt beard and dirtied cheeks stands there. He's dressed in tattered pants and a long-sleeved shirt. His clothes are covered in stains and dirt. He holds up a sign, reading SUGAR-MOMMA WANTED. He's not holding it up for me, but at the two older women nearby admiring a sculpture made of blown colored glass. One clutches her pearl necklace. The other shakes her head in contempt.

The man laughs, gives a toothless smile, then spits. The loogie drips down the glass over the stenciled letters of the gallery's name. He starts screaming, "Fucking bitches! All you crones don't know what you're missing." He grabs his crotch, crushes it into the window, then flips us off.

The gallery owner groans. I imagine it's not the highlight of her day to go outside and clean throat phlegm off the glass.

"The homeless are a real problem here," one of the women says to the other. "Someone should do something about them."

"Tell me about it," her companion says.

I hate to admit it to myself, but part of me is quick to agree. If I'm being truly honest, when I first saw him, there was a sense of revulsion. Of wanting to avoid him. Of wanting him to go away so I didn't have to look at him.

All through my life, I've encountered those hanging out at intersections, begging for change or food. Those sleeping on sidewalks, making others walk around them. Those pushing stolen grocery carts along the sides of roads.

Outside the window, the burly man crosses the street without looking either way, and he's nearly hit by a truck. He smashes his hands on the hood of the vehicle and screams at the driver. Then he keeps walking, harassing anyone in his path.

I wonder where he's going, how he eats, where he sleeps.

Technically, I don't have four walls to protect me from the outside world. I don't have a kitchen or a fridge or cabinets full of food. I don't have a bathroom where I can shower as long as I want. I don't have a place to rest my head. Not anymore.

The homeless are unpleasant to look at. But I never thought about why.

Maybe it's cause the only thing separating *us* from *them* is a twist of fate. A wrong turn. A streak of bad luck.

Only now . . . when I look at him, the shame runs deeper. Cause I'm not so unlike him. I'm not part of *us* anymore. I'm more like *them*.

second date

know this hole-in-the-wall restaurant. You're going to love it,"
Russell says, closing the door to his Jeep.

"Is it expensive?" I ask, trying not to worry.

"Nah, it's a local hangout. It's dirt-cheap," he says, reversing
out of his driveway. "Don't worry. I'll let you save your nickels
and dimes for college tuition."

Nickels and dimes have never seemed so valuable as
they do now.

After parking, Russell takes me around a fleet of shops to a
side street. The faded yellow sign says simply TACO. A beaded
curtain attempts to block the small AC from leaking its precious
cool air outside. Inside, a small black-and-white TV plays from
a perch near the ceiling. The red walls are decorated with
burning hearts and Virgin Marys. There're only two tables,
both occupied, and a young woman nods for Russell to go to
the back. On the way, we pass the kitchen, where an old woman
is crafting tortillas with her bare hands and a rolling pin. She

listens to a small radio playing Tejano music. It makes me long for my own abuela. I follow Russell out into a garden area with more tables and more patrons. There's a table for two in the far-left corner.

"You're going to love this place," he says. "Authentic as hell. You're going to go wild for the food."

The young woman arrives with a small basket of chips and salsa. She points to a wrinkled paper menu already on the table. It lists simply: *pollo, carnitas, carne, cerveza,* and *tequila.*

"Ready?" she asks, her voice tinted by a Mexican accent.

Russell holds up two fingers, saying, "Two of everything on the menu." The waitress disappears into the back kitchen. "You have to try one of everything. We can order more if you're still hungry."

The woman reappears a few minutes later. She deposits two bottles of Corona in front of us, then adds two shot glasses. She pours sloppily from a bottle with a small worm floating inside it. She doesn't bother to look at me or ask my age.

A slice of lime juts out of each bottle mouth. Russell squeezes his into the glass, presses the lime down, then seals the glass with his thumb and turns it upside down, then right side up. He waits for me to do the same. He holds up his shot glass. "Ready?"

"Ready," I say.

"Salud," he says. Takes his shot, and then swigs the beer.

"Salud," I repeat. Taking my shot, but careful to sip, careful not to make the same mistake I did last night. Though the shot calls that into question. I haven't eaten since my Cheerios breakfast.

"So how was your day?"

"I wandered around the French Quarter."

"That place is a tourist trap."

"I kind of love it."

"Oh, it's pretty enough, but most locals avoid it."

"You ever go to Bourbon Street?"

"Once in a blue moon," Russell says. "When I'm feeling wild."

"Do you go to the . . . you know . . ."

"The gay bars?" Russell lowers his voice, leaning in. He smiles. "Hell, yeah. You need to go to Southern Decadence with me. End of summer. It's amazing."

"What's that?"

"It's a circuit party. The whole event lasts for days. Dancing, drinking, making out with strangers—if you're into that, that is. It's the best time."

"Have you ever . . ."

"Kissed a stranger? Well, I kissed you in that hotel lobby."

"Yeah, I remember."

Russell's foot finds mine under the table and rubs my leg. Above the table, he grins. "Best decision I ever made."

"You hardly know me."

"So help me get to know you. Tell me everything."

I want to. I do. But I can't. Instead, I say, "I'm not that interesting."

"Try me."

"Where should I start?"

Russell takes another swig of his beer and says, "Start at the beginning."

"Well . . . I was born in Abilene, Texas. Soon after, we moved to Guam and Okinawa, cause my dad was Air Force. We moved back when I was four, and my parents got a divorce not too long after that. I grew up all over Texas. We moved a lot."

"Why?"

"My mom and stepdad weren't so good at keeping their jobs."

"Were they good parents?"

I can't help but wince. I find myself taking a swig of my own beer. "Not really."

"That was loaded," Russell notes. "Bad childhood?"

"You could say that. They were pretty generous with the fists. That's why I don't want to go back there. To Texas, I mean."

"I'm sorry," Russell says. "That's rough. My dad was pretty hard on us too. He didn't hesitate to take his belt off when we were kids. Whipped us 'til we couldn't sit. At least, until he got sober. He's been sober over a decade. Now he's a pretty decent father."

It feels like I've been punched in the stomach. Just thinking of my own dad. Of what happened only a few days ago.

I take another swig of beer.

"Where'd you go?" Russell asks.

"Huh?"

"You disappeared there for a second. What's the story with your dad?"

"I moved in with him after I graduated from high school. He left when I was five, so I wanted to get to know him better. Turns out that was a mistake."

"How come?"

I swallow another swig of beer. I need a minute to come up with a lie. Or a half-truth. Something that doesn't give away everything. I stop myself from taking another gulp of beer. Already my head feels a little swimmy. Maybe from the shot. I need to slow down. But I don't want to feel this. I want to dull the pain. To fall asleep in Russell's arms again.

"What about your mom?" I ask. "Is she nice?"

Russell doesn't press me about my dad. "Yeah, she's great," he says. "I came out to her a few years ago. At first things were a little rocky, what with her being Catholic and all. But she caved after a few months."

"Wow."

"Yeah. I'm lucky. I take it you haven't told your parents?"

I bring the lip of the bottle to my mouth, sucking it down 'til it's gone.

"Whoa. You might wanna slow down there, cowboy."

"My dad found out," I whisper. "It wasn't good."

"How bad was it?"

My eyes brim with tears. I try to pull them back. Shove them down. But it doesn't work. A tear drips down my cheek.

That's when the food arrives.

I wipe my tear away with the butt of my palm.

"Rex—" Russell says.

"Can we talk about it later?" I ask.

Russell nods.

I take a bite of my taco. The warm juices of the meat caress my mouth as I chew. "You're right," I say, sniffling. "This is good."

Russell bites his lip, no doubt noticing my forced smile.

————

After dinner, we walk. His shoulder brushes mine. He says, "I wish I could hold your hand like we were a normal couple. But this neighborhood—"

"I know," I say. "It's okay."

"You wanna finish telling me what happened back there in the restaurant?"

"I'm really embarrassed right now."

"There's nothing to be embarrassed about. Coming out? It's not easy. At least not for most people. Some parents don't take it well. And some—"

And suddenly—suddenly I'm crying.

Russell stops us. He puts his hands on my shoulders and tries to look at my down-turned eyes. "What is it?"

"I don't want to lie to you," I say, some of my words coming out in a slur. "But I don't want to be honest either. You'll hate me."

"Hate you for what? What are you talking about?"

I sit on the curb, holding my face in my hands. "My dad kicked me out."

Russell sits on the curb next to me. "What?"

"My dad found out I was gay. He disowned me. He kicked me out."

"When?"

I hesitate.

"Wait, is that why you're here?"

I nod.

"Who are you staying with?"

Then I'm sobbing.

"No one."

"Where'd you sleep the night before?"

"My truck."

"Oh, Rex." Then he does the opposite of what I expect him to do. He kisses me. My lips wet with tears, pressed against his. After a minute, he whispers, "Shhhh. It's going to be okay."

"Is it?" I ask.

"It is," he says. And he hugs me tight.

———

He turns on the light in his living room. I'm still sniffling, trying to inhale the snot so it doesn't drip out of my nose. "You have a tissue?"

"Toilet paper work?"

Once in the bathroom, I close the door. I stare at myself in the mirror. I'm a mess. Flushed skin and red-eyed from crying. I splash cold water on my face. As I dry myself, I inhale Russell's scent from the towel. Why's he being so nice to me?

When I come out, he asks, "Where's your stuff?"

"My truck."

"Go get it. You're crashing here tonight."

"Russell, I can't."

"Yes, you can."

"No, seriously. It's fine."

"It's not fine. Go get your stuff."

"You sure?"

"I'm sure."

When I come back inside with my duffel and backpack, Russell is standing at the bathroom with a folded white towel. "Why don't you shower, get yourself cleaned up, so you can sleep?"

My muscles tighten, nerves activating, worrying he's going to pressure me into sex. I barely know him. Though if I'm being honest, every time he kisses me I think about getting him naked. I want to, but the situation is so new. I don't know what's the right choice.

Sheepishly, I ask, "Where am I going to sleep?"

"Wherever you want," Russell says. "You can sleep in bed with me. Or on the futon if you're more comfortable there. It folds out."

"Thanks," I say, feeling some calm coming over me.

The shower feels like heaven. It's so hot out that I turn the temperature down 'til the water is cool on my skin. Then I brush my teeth, change into fresh underwear, gym shorts, and a tank top. When I come out, Russell is making up the futon bed. Clean sheets, a pillow, even a blanket. "In case you get cold," he says.

"Thanks," I say. "But you don't have to—"

"I know I don't. But I want to. You're in a bad situation. I'm not about to make you go sleep in the streets. Not after what your dad did. I'm not asking you to move in or anything. But we can figure out the details later. Not tonight."

I lay down on the futon, pull the sheet up, feel the gentle stir of the air conditioner blowing over me. Turns out I do need the blanket.

Russell kisses my forehead and says good night. After he turns out the lights and gets into his bed, I toss and turn for an hour.

Even under the blanket, I'm cold. I'm shaking. But it's not the temperature. It's everything else, all of it, my whole life crashing down on top of me, threatening to smother me, to snuff me out. I don't have anywhere to go. I don't have a safe space. I don't have a home. I want to scream and fight and run away, but instead I'm frozen. Wondering if I'll ever have family or friends again.

I look through the sliding doors into the bedroom. I stare at Russell while he lies there. I want to cry, he's being so nice to me. And he doesn't even know me.

Then Russell opens his eyes.

"Can't sleep?" he asks.

I shake my head.

He scoots over, lifting the sheets and blanket in front of him. "Come here."

I hesitate.

"We don't have to have sex," he says. "But maybe some cuddling will make you feel better."

I don't want to be alone.

So I get up, and tiptoe over to his bed, and crawl in next to him.

———

I'm dreaming of one thing, but feeling something else. My lips and tongue are moving. My body presses against another warm body. The heat between us is addictive, so I push into it. Rolling out of the dream and into the waking world is so subtle I barely notice, until I open my eyes and realize I'm making out with Russell.

I don't know if he started it or if I did, but I don't want it to stop. His arms and legs are wrapped around me as my hands explore his body. He pulls off my shirt, then I take the lead, tugging off his shorts and underwear. Mine come off too.

I keep kissing him, but hold back. Cause I don't want to rush into anything. My head, logic, throws up boundaries that I shouldn't cross. Yet the more we kiss, the more our bodies grind into one another, the more I want it to give in. Some deep and basic instinct pulls me out of my head and into my body, into some ingrained imperative that drives me, leads my every move. Until it's all I want. Cause this *is* what I want. This is what I've wanted since I first saw Russell in the ocean. And I don't want to deny it. Not anymore.

———

The next morning, I sleepily crawl out of bed, put on my gym shorts, and walk into the kitchen. Russell is sitting at the table, clothed in nothing but a pair of white briefs, eating a bowl of Cheerios.

"Good morning, Sexy Rexy," he says, grinning from ear to ear like the Cheshire cat. He pulls my face down to kiss me, and I kiss him back. Just smelling him makes my whole body come alive as we press into each other. "Last night was amazing."

"You were amazing," I say.

"I've never—*never*—felt that way before. It was the best sex I've ever had," Russell says. And then we're kissing again.

———

I'm sitting up on the futon, basking in the glow of last night. And again this morning.

I can smell Russell on myself, on my chest and arms and hands. I keep inhaling his musk on my skin. My thoughts replay the scenes over and over and over. I've never been this happy.

When Russell comes out of the bathroom, he's wearing his brown uniform. "I gotta get to work."

"Noooooo," I whine. "Call in sick. Stay home."

"I have to go in. I need to make that money."

"Okay. Give me five minutes and I'll be ready to go."

"Don't bother. Stay."

"What do you mean?"

Russell smiles. "I'll go to work. You chill here. And I'll

be back before you know it. Help yourself to whatever's in the fridge."

"Russell. I should really leave."

"And go where?" he asks.

I can't think of anything to say, so I say nothing.

"But I'm basically a stranger."

"Not after last night, you aren't." Russell pulls me off the futon, and we're kissing again. "Plus, I want to spend more time with you."

"Really?"

"Really," he says, his voice genuine. "Why don't you stay here for a little while? Just 'til you get back on your feet."

"I have no idea how long that'll take."

"Then we'll worry about that later. For now, we'll take it one day at a time."

"Russell, come on. You really don't have to—"

"But I want to." He kisses me on the nose. "I like you, Rex. I really like you. And I want to spend more time with you. I want you to stay."

I don't have any other place to go.

And, truthfully? I don't want to leave.

So I kiss him back, and say, "Okay."

my plan

I turn on the radio, and dance around Russell's living room. A lightness has overtaken me and I feel like I can breathe. For the first time in days, I'm not so scared of the future.

Russell wants me to stay, at least for a little while. It'll give me time to figure things out. But I'm not going to waste any time.

I eat a bowl of cereal. I brush my teeth. I count my money. Already there isn't much left. I try not to think about that.

I make Russell's bed. Then I fold the sheets and blanket on the futon, and adjust it back into a couch. I wash the dishes in his sink, putting them in the drying rack. Even with the AC running it's still warm inside. I take a shower to cool off.

Once I'm dressed, I eat some of the deli meat in Russell's fridge. I don't want to be greedy, so I only take two slices of turkey. I grab a banana for later. That's going to be my lunch today.

I grab the spare key Russell left for me, and lock the door as I head outside. Heat blasts me in the face like a furnace, the air like hot soup. Barely one block walking, and already I'm sweating through my shirt.

But I have a plan in mind.

First, I'm going to get a job. Second, I'm going to find a place to live. Third, I'm going to apply to colleges, and get in. Heck, if I can get into college, I can live in a dorm. Two birds, one stone. It's all so doable. This is my plan. I'm going to start over. I'm going to be like a cat, landing on my feet after a fall. Everything's going to be okay.

Step one, then. Find a job.

It should be easy. I've never not worked. I've earned money doing this and that since I was ten years old.

First, babysitting for a neighbor. Then, babysitting for all my neighbors until nearly every night was scheduled. When I turned fifteen, I got a job at Anderson's Video Rental off the highway. When I was sixteen, I started busing tables and restocking the pantries and freezer at Abilene's Pizza and Spaghetti Warehouse. Then, when I moved to Alabama, I got the job at Walmart.

Walmart. My last job, wearing a blue vest, pushing shopping carts from the parking lot to the inside of the store, and unpacking boxes to stock the shelves. It wasn't a great job, but I certainly didn't hate it. And I made friends. We weren't that close, but if not for them I would never have met Russell.

But Alabama is behind me. I can't go back, even if I wanted to. And I don't.

Not really.

Even if I do miss Rebecca and Mona. Even if I miss my dad.

I don't know why. I can't explain it. How I can love and hate someone so much at the same time. After what he did to me, I'm so furious. Scared, sure, but angry at him. I'm so mad that he couldn't step up and be a more accepting father.

Yet, still, I want us to be okay. He's the only dad I have.

Had.

Past tense.

Shaking my head, I try to banish thoughts of my old life. I can't think of that right now. It's too soon. And it's done. I can't change what happened now.

I have to move forward.

Today I'm going to apply to every single job I can find. It doesn't matter what the position is. Server, barista, cashier, whatever. I've heard it's always easier to get a job once you have a job. So I just need something—anything—first. I can upgrade later. Maybe I can even get two jobs, and really save up some cash.

As I walk along, the sun hangs in the sky overhead, baking the sidewalk. I pass a homeless man, his bare feet blistered and scabbed. I don't know why, but he's wearing a sweater. He couldn't possibly be cold, could he? His hair is matted into dirty clumps, his fingernails black with grime. As I pass, he asks for money.

I say, "I'm sorry," and keep moving.

The first business I come across is a coffee shop. I walk in, finding myself halfway between shy and aggressive. I need this, but I'm also not sure if I'm qualified. The aroma of fresh coffee scents the air. It's pleasant, even with the sounds of machines making steam.

"What can I get you?" the young woman asks from behind the register.

"Oh, um, yeah, I was wondering if you're hiring."

"You have to speak to the manager. Hold on." She disappears into a backroom.

When the manager comes out, she says, "We're fully staffed at the moment, but thanks for coming in."

I walk into the next business, a shop selling candles. Not hiring either.

I walk into the next business, a restaurant. The hostess is annoyed. "You have to come back between three and five. We're dealing with the lunch rush right now."

The next place is a corner store. There isn't any availability, but they'll let me fill out an application in case anything opens up. They hand me an application. I pull out *Interview with the Vampire*, and use it as a hard surface to write on. I fill out my name. Just below is a request for my address and phone number. I don't know what to put.

I don't have an address or a phone number.

It feels like a punch in the gut.

Such a simple request. Forms I've filled out dozens of times before. And I always took it for granted. Until now. Now that I don't have an address or a landline to call my own.

I don't know what to put.

I guess I could put down Russell's information. But I don't want to make any assumptions. I mean, surely he wants me to get a job, so I can get my own place. He wouldn't mind. Would he?

I write it down. Then I fill out my employment history. That looks good. I've been employed before, lots of times. Though when the application asks for addresses and phone numbers for everywhere I've worked, I realize I don't have that. The next section asks for references. I don't have those either. And I can't use Walmart. I stopped showing up out of nowhere. I didn't even call.

"Stupid." I hit myself in the head with my fist. How could I be so dumb? I wasn't prepared for this. I don't know what to do.

If I turn in an unfinished application, they'll toss it. I need a job. I need money. I need to take care of myself.

Maybe if I explain my situation?

But, telling my story? The real honest truth? That would mean admitting my dad kicked me out for being gay. What if they don't hire me cause of that? My stomach turns. I could always lie. But if they caught me lying, I'd never get a job there.

I fill out what I can on the application. When I go inside to return it, I tell the manager, "I don't have all the addresses and phone numbers of places I've worked, cause I just moved here, but I really need a job. Hire me and you won't be sorry."

"We'll see if anything comes available," he says. Then he turns and walks away.

I keep moving. I walk the main streets. I stop anywhere that's open. Another coffee shop. A bakery. A grocery store. A donut shop. A record store. A video store. An arcade. An auto-repair service. An electronics store. A hardware store. A magazine stand.

"We're fully staffed."

"We're not hiring."

"Fill out an application and we'll call you if anything opens up."

Sitting under the shade of a tree, I try to ignore the pain in my gut. I'm not sure if I'm hungry, or simply stressed. I pull the banana out of my backpack and eat it.

At three in the afternoon, I retrace my steps. I float along the heated sidewalk, trying to stick to the shade of the infrequent trees. I wipe my sweating brow, hitting up all the restaurants I passed earlier. Now that the lunch rush is done, I can apply. But again, I hear a lot of the same:

"We're fully staffed."

"We're not hiring."

"Fill out an application and we'll call you if anything opens up."

Until one manager says, "We need a busboy."

"Absolutely," I say. "I'm in."

"Fill this out and we'll look over it with the other applications. We'll call you."

Luckily, the next three restaurants are hiring. A waiter, a host, a food runner. I apply to all of them, which is followed by a "We'll call you."

"Why is it so hard to find a job?" I whisper to myself while I'm filling out another application.

The hostess overhears me, and answers, "Lots of locals scoop up all the good stuff. Once they have a job, they hang on to it. Same with the college kids. It's a big city, but it has more people than work."

I try not to let my heart sink. I'm young. I'm smart. I should be able to find something. It just takes time. I have to keep trying. And today's only my first day looking. It'll be fine.

It'll be fine.

I'll get a job.

These things just take time.

———

For the rest of the week, I expand my search. I go into more stores and shops and restaurants. I keep smiling, asking politely if they're hiring. And I keep filling out applications, spotted with blank spaces, holes of missing information, hoping that it won't matter.

Even though I suspect it will.

the man

can't waste any gas, cause I can't afford to fill up the tank. So I don't use my truck to search for jobs. I just keep walking farther and farther from Russell's, in different directions, trying to find new places to apply to.

But on Friday, by five-thirty I'm back at Russell's, exhausted and more than a little dehydrated. I take off my shoes and socks and rub my sore feet until I fall asleep on the couch. When he gets home at six, Russell furrows his brow. "You been sleeping all day?"

"Of course not. I applied for more jobs."

"Where?"

"Pretty much every place I came across."

"Right," he mumbles, taking off his work shirt.

"I really have been trying. I've filled out probably a hundred applications. I just need one of them to call me back."

"How are they going to contact you?"

"I wrote down your phone number."

Russell looks pissed off.

"Should I not have done that?"

"You should've asked me first."

"Sorry."

"Whatever." Then he disappears into the bathroom. I hear the shower turn on.

Guilt punishes my stomach. I did what I could, but maybe I'm not doing enough. I already feel like a mooch, what with Russell paying for everything. Groceries, rent, utilities. I need to get a job. Sooner rather than later.

I'm sitting on the edge of the bed when Russell comes out in a towel. I say, "I really am trying."

"I know," Russell says. He crosses the room and kisses me. "I just had a bad day at work. I shouldn't take it out on you."

"It's okay. I should have asked you about using your phone number. I just didn't know what else to do."

"It's fine," he says, lips curling into a grin. "How could someone not want to hire someone so cute?"

"You're the cute one," I say.

We kiss again.

"You want to make it up to me?" Russell says.

"What'd you have in mind?"

"Well, first you can cook dinner for me. Then you can give me a long massage. And then after that . . ." His eyes turn mischievous.

"I can do all of that," I say, leading him into the kitchen. I start looking through the cabinets and the fridge, even though I already know what's in there. "How about omelets and toast?"

"Breakfast for dinner? I'm down. As long as you can make an omelet."

"I can flip it and everything."

"This I gotta see," he says, wrapping his arms around my waist as I pull eggs, butter, and cheese from the fridge.

As I start cooking, Russell opens a beer and starts drinking. He watches me until I say, "What?"

"Just admiring you," he says. "I like seeing you in my kitchen, making me dinner. Like a good wife."

I throw a hand towel at him playfully. "You're the wife."

"No, I'm the breadwinner. That makes me the man."

I can't argue with that. So I give him a kiss and say, "You're the man."

inside

From Russell's front door, you can see the back door. There's no hallway, just one door leading into the next room, leading into the next room. The living room, the kitchen, the bedroom, the bathroom, and the back room. Russell says it's called a shotgun layout.

When I asked why it was called that, he said, "That way if you stand at the front door, you could shoot someone in the back room."

I asked, "Who's shooting people from the front door?"

Russell shrugged. "That's just what it's called."

It made me laugh.

Though, right now? I don't feel like laughing. I want to go outside. But I'm stuck waiting by Russell's phone.

Any minute, someone could call and offer me a job interview. Or even better, a job. I want to be here to answer when they do. I'm getting desperate. I need work. All I need is one employer to call me back.

Just one.

I clean Russell's house. I dust every surface. I vacuum the wooden floor and use the tube to get the corners and under the furniture. I wipe the counters and make sure the kitchen sink is empty of dishes. I even clean the bathroom. Shower, sink, toilet. All the while listening for the phone. Finally, I sit on Russell's futon. Waiting.

The house felt so big the first week I was here. The high ceilings. The tall windows. The shotgun layout. Russell's presence.

But when Russell's at work, I feel like the last person in the world. Like nothing outside exists. No cities. No people. Just this one house. A prison cell.

As I sit here, the ceiling feels lower. The living room walls seem to lean in. I want to open a window, but Russell asked me to keep them all closed, to keep the sunlight and the heat out. Still, the AC struggles to combat the humidity. And with the windows closed, the front rooms are dark. The bedroom is darker. And the back room, windowless, the darkest. The shotgun layout reminds me of a tunnel, leading farther and farther into a well of night.

I turn on the TV. I flip channels for a while. Watching bits and parts of daytime talk shows, soap operas, and the news. Finally, I settle on MTV. They're playing a marathon of *The Real World: Miami.* "This is the true story of seven strangers, picked to live in a house . . ."

Seven young men and women, some only a little older than me, chose to leave the comfort of their homes and go to a new house. Just like me. Except they weren't forced to do it. They moved for fun. To get on TV. To be famous. Me? No one knows who I am. No one except Russell.

It dawns on me that he's the only person I know in this whole city. In Alabama I knew dozens of people, mostly coworkers, but still. In Texas I went to a school of two thousand. I wasn't popular or anything, but I knew a lot of people. I had neighbors. I had family. Even if they were awful. I still had people.

Here . . . no one would know if something *bad* happened to me.

An ache starts to crawl through my body. It starts behind my shoulders, in the center of my upper back. It's just a flutter, not of pain, exactly, but not *not* pain. It's something else. Like stress, only it hurts more.

Soon it's contagious. Catching in my other muscles. Even the flesh beneath my skin starts to gnaw at me. I try rubbing my arms, legs, shoulders. It doesn't help. I have to stop myself from grinding my teeth. My whole body throbs, from toe to head. Like something is washing through it, some biological panic.

I'm so angry and scared, I want to fight, I want to run. But who would I battle? Where would I go? I need to wait here. By the phone. Just in case . . .

But it dawns on me, I have to move. It's worse if I just sit here.

So I force myself to stand. And I pace. The light-colored wood creaks underfoot as I walk the length of the living room. I put one foot in front of the other, trying to perfectly line up heel to toe. I count as I cross the room. Then I turn around and do it again. And again. As if the outcome will change.

It doesn't.

I keep pacing, counting, breathing, until the ache lessens. It doesn't go away. It's just not as bad. Like I remembered myself.

At the front window, I peek outside. There's a few feet of grass and flowers, and then the street lined with trees. Across the road is a row of buildings. Some are more long shotgun homes, the others are full-on houses. One is a two-story. It doesn't look well kept, but not quite falling apart yet. Painted white, with black trim. Vines overgrow one side, clinging to the wall, the way babies cling to their parents. I wish that I were a baby again. That someone would take care of me. That I could start over. But I can't.

This is my life now.

Waiting in a dark house, staring at a phone, trying to will it to ring.

It doesn't.

circles

When Russell walks into the kitchen, I look up from my cereal bowl and say, "There's my sexy man in uniform."

"Yeah?"

"Yeah," I say. "I would whistle at you, but I don't know how."

"Baby doesn't know how to whistle?" Russell hugs me, and whistles in my ear, then he starts kissing my neck up and down. I start to unbuckle his belt, but he pushes my hands away. "I want to, trust me, but that would make me late for work. Again."

"You didn't mind being late yesterday."

"My boss sure did."

"Fine," I say, backing off. "I'll behave."

Russell takes me in, surveying me toe to head. "Damn, kid. You're killing me." He plants his lips on mine. Then says, "Oh yeah, I have something for you."

"You do?"

Russell hands me a thick Sunday newspaper. "I know the

job search isn't panning out, so I thought you could check out the Employment section. Maybe there's something there."

I don't know why I didn't think of that. It makes me feel stupid and guilty at the same time. I kiss Russell and say, "Thanks."

"Maybe you can get a job as a secretary." He raises his eyebrows. "Or a sex phone operator."

"Har har," I say.

Russell barks at me. I can't help but laugh.

But as the door closes after him, like every day lately, my mood drops. When he leaves, it's like the sun goes out of the room, and I'm left behind, alone in my head with my dangerous thoughts. I keep replaying my last days in Alabama. I keep considering the uncertainty of the future. I worry that I won't get a job. That Russell will tire of me, get sick of me. That he'll tell me to leave. Then where will I go?

No, I can't think about that.

I fish around in the miscellaneous drawer in the kitchen until I find a red pen. Then I lay out the newspaper on the floor. I read over the descriptions, circling job after job that I think I could do. But they want résumés, which I don't have. They want someone with work attire, which I don't have. They want years of job experience, which I don't have.

It takes every ounce of restraint not to crumple up the newspaper and throw it across the room.

The ache starts to well up inside me again. My head swims with pain. My stomach twists over and over. It's just stress, I tell myself. But it's not just that. Every time I think of my intended plan, it feels impossible. I need a job. I need my own place. I need to get back into school. The more my thoughts spiral, the more it feels like a weight is crushing me.

Like my body has some terrible warning system, and it's trying to warn me that everything is falling apart.

No. I shake my head. It's going to be okay. It's going to be okay.

It has to be.

My skin crawls, and I'm ready to jump out of it. I find myself pacing again, in circles, trying to calm my thoughts. I place my feet down with purpose, stepping heel to toe, heel to toe, as if a controlled walk will give me some control over the rest of my life. But it helps me think.

Okay, revisit the plan. Maybe I should go to all the places I've applied for jobs and remind them about me. Maybe they'll appreciate my persistence. Or maybe it will annoy them. Maybe I should skip a step and go to a local college campus and see if I can apply for late admission. Maybe I should turn around and go back to Alabama.

No. I'm not doing that. I won't bow down to my father. I refuse.

And Russell's here. I don't want to leave him. He's the only thing in my life that feels right.

But I need help.

I think of my abuela. She's always been there for me. She knows what it's like to do without. She came from Mexico, born into poverty. She crossed the border into Texas to clean houses and save up money. She met my grandfather, married, and had five children, before her husband died in Vietnam. Once again, she found herself with next to nothing. She took a risk, moved her family from Kansas to Texas, where she found a community at both church and Abilene Christian University.

But I don't have a faith to lean into. I wish I did. I just

don't believe in god. I mean, I don't think there's some old man with a big beard sitting up on a golden throne in the clouds, condemning people to hell or sending them up to heaven. But every time I think of religion, I think back to going to church with Abuela. Driving up to her church, we could see a huge sign that read GAY IS SIN, AND SIN IS AN AFFRONT TO GOD. And the sermon called out Leviticus 18:22, saying a man lying with another man was an abomination. The pastor went on to say those who were gay would burn in hell. Their immortal souls condemned to suffer. For eternity.

I find myself wondering, Maybe there is a god. Maybe he is punishing me. Maybe he has a terrible fate in store for me for making the choice I did. Maybe I should have caved. Maybe my dad was right.

No.

I can't accept that. I refuse to go back. I refuse to beg for help. I just wish I didn't feel so lost right now.

There's always been one person I could talk to, who would make me feel better, my whole life she was there for me. Maybe if I just heard her voice it would make me feel better. I don't have to tell her anything. I could just call . . .

I pick up the phone, and I stare at it for a long time.

I know her number by heart.

I dial.

The phone rings. Rings again. And again.

Her answering machine finally picks up.

But I can't bring myself to leave a message. What would I even say? "I'm gay. I'm homeless. I'm scared." I can't do it. I think of all the Sunday mornings and Wednesday nights she spends at her church. She loves her religion, and her god. And in their eyes, gay is wrong. It's a sin. And I don't want Abuela to look at me and see a demon.

I don't want her to see me that way.

So I hang up.

Outside the window is the rest of the world. The pastel houses and the colorful folks who live inside them. Farther down the streets, tourists take in the sights, locals leave their jobs to go to lunch. And here I am, locked inside like Rapunzel. Except no one locked me away. This is a self-imposed exile, while I try to save every dime, try to find a job, try not to feel desperately alone.

I miss my stepsister. I miss watching TV with her. Going to the movies. Laughing at our parents behind their backs.

The clock on the wall says it's only three in the afternoon. My dad should be at work. Mona too. But Rebecca should be home.

I dial the number

She says, "Hello?"

"It's me."

"Rex?"

"Yeah."

"Oh my god. Are you okay?!"

I don't even know how to answer that. Physically, I'm fine. Except for the ache inside me that won't go away except when I'm with Russell. Mentally, I'm exhausted, and terrified. Spiritually? It feels like I've fallen away from my life. Like I'm lost.

"Rex, are you there? Tell me you're okay."

"I'm here," I whisper. Sniffling.

Then I'm crying.

Then my sister is crying with me.

vampires

Russell and I are walking down Coliseum Street to go to dinner.

His shoulder bumps into my shoulder playfully. His fingers tickle mine as they swing by. He glances over often to bark at me. After long days alone inside, it feels good to be outside with Russell, taking in the open night sky.

Passing a cemetery, I can't help but notice how haunting it is, yet so beautiful at the same time. It's like a small city of markers and tombs made of marble and concrete, dirtied by centuries of weather and lack of care.

I ask, "Why are all the graves aboveground?"

"To prevent coffins from rising out of the dirt when it's too wet," Russell says. "The water table is too high in N'awlins, so nothing buried stays underground for long. Things float to the top."

I shiver at the thought of no longer living. I don't want to spend eternity in a box, below- or aboveground. I ask, "You ever wanted to be a vampire?"

"No way," Russell says. "The sight of blood makes me queasy."

"So why do you order your burgers so rare?"

"That's different. Those are cows. I'm talking human blood."

"I don't care. I want to be a vampire."

"Why?"

"So I can live forever. So I can't be hurt anymore."

"Won't it hurt when people you love die?"

"I guess so."

"Plus, there's the whole-stake-through-the-heart-and-sword-to-chop-off-your-head stuff."

"True. But I'll keep a low profile, and I'll only drink animal blood. I won't hurt actual people."

"You say that now . . . but I've seen your bloodlust. Well, your lust for me anyways. You wouldn't be able to resist biting me."

I play-push Russell.

"Is that why you read all those lady books?" Russell asks.

"What lady books?"

"Anne Rice."

"Those aren't lady books."

"If you say so," Russell says. Then adds, "You been to her house yet?"

"Her house?"

"Yeah. She lives in the Garden District, not far from here. They have tours that go through her place."

I go light-headed. I've always wanted to meet her. But now my mind races with the idea of going on the tour, of meeting her in the flesh, of her being drawn to me cause we're kindred souls. Our eyes would lock, and we'd be drawn together like two magnets, like two characters from one of her books. Then she would ask me to come live with her, ask if she could adopt me as her own. It's so unlikely, but I can't shake the fantasy of having a new family.

————

The next day, I put on khaki shorts and my favorite shirt. I'm giddy with excitement, that today might be the day I meet Anne Rice. And the fantasy of her adopting me feels real. It feels possible. Like there's a reason for everything, and this is why the universe brought me to New Orleans. To start new with a mother who I adore and loves me in return.

I step outside, take a breath of the fresh air, and stride toward a home I've only dreamt of . . . the house on 1314 Napoleon Avenue.

When I see the exterior for the first time, there is a pull in my soul. Both unsteady and steadfast, I move closer. A wrought-iron gate separates the three-story home from the street. Taking up an entire city block, the building is red brick on either side, but painted white at the center, with black shutters and eight columns. I remember a young Deirdre fleeing to this house in Anne Rice's Mayfair Witches series. A sign over the door reads ST. ELIZABETH'S, to match the name on the Historic Landmark plaque stating that this used to be an orphanage for children.

The burly tour guide welcomes the small crowd. He says the cost of the tour is ten dollars. Even with so little money left, I hand over the cash without hesitation. I am ready to go inside.

Two stone angels stand on either side of the stairs, as if

welcoming me to a safe haven. The front porch's Corinthian columns guard bare brick walls, elegant draperies, mirrors, and chandeliers. In the entry, we pass an old Victrola record player and a Saint Elizabeth statue. Soon after, I walk through a library overflowing with books. Antiques and artwork populate every room, including one that houses a massive collection of hundreds of dolls, whose eyes seem to stare back. Stained-glass windows illuminate a chapel with a wooden dance floor for balls.

Any moment I expect to turn the corner and run into Anne Rice herself. That is, until the tour guide informs us that the famous author actually resides in her other home on First Street.

My soul feels crushed. However unlikely, I honestly thought fate would bring me together with the writer I love so much. That we were destined to meet. That we might be swept up together in some secret world of vampires and witches and immortals that view me as special, unique enough to turn me into one of them.

But that's not going to happen now.

It was silly of me to think so.

I try not to pout. I try to stay in the present and appreciate all the magic of this house, but I can't focus. I can't shake the thought that the universe is purposely working against me. Cause I am unable to get out of my own head, the tour is over too fast.

After, I find myself standing outside, staring back at one of Anne Rice's two homes, wishing that I just had one.

dancing

'm standing awkwardly in the corner, taking sips of ginger ale. Russell is on the dance floor, waving me over. I motion that I'm fine where I am.

Thump thump thump. The bass of the music drums through my whole body, punishing my ears. The darkness of the club is split up by rays of light. Red, green, white flashes off the disco ball until a strobe takes effect. The hiss of a smoke machine goes off, and puffs of white waft over the crowd before sinking to the floor. Across the dance floor, a sea of shirtless men undulate and rock side to side like trees swept up in a storm. They kick their feet and punch the air to the rhythm of the beat. It's tribal and beautiful.

I can't help but admire the freedom of the crowd within these walls, when outside is a world that doesn't want us to be ourselves.

Russell sways over, his white teeth whiter under the black lights. He shouts in my ear, "Come dance."

"I'm not a good dancer."

"No one's a good dancer," he shouts back. Grabbing my hand, he drags me into the middle of the throng. At first I just stand there, feeling foolish. He takes my hands and starts moving from left to right and back. I roll my eyes. But his laughter is infectious. Before I know it, I'm dancing alongside him. When his lips are on mine, electricity passes through us.

I don't know why he likes me. Why he's letting me stay with him. Why he's feeding me when I have no way to repay him. But at the moment I try not to care. I let the questions slide away, as our bodies press together and move in tandem with the sounds and vibrations of our gay congregation.

We dance for hours.

When we finally walk outside, the air is hot and sticky. Our shirts cling to our bodies, soaked through with sweat. We get in Russell's Jeep, and he kisses me. We drive home with dawn looming on the horizon. Plunging into bed, we pull one another's clothes off. Our lips locked. Everything is so intense. So raw. When it's just him and me, naked in bed, everything feels right. I feel so close to him. Like our bodies have melded. Like there's no past and no future. There's just now. Like I don't have a care in the world.

He stares into my eyes. His lips part. They tremble ever so slightly. Hesitant, building some powerful tension between us. And then the words spill out.

"I love you, Rex."

I'm caught off guard.

We've known each other for such a short time.

Yet we've already spent so many hours together, had so

many conversations, given one another so much, in ways I never imagined two people could.

His words pierce me. Words, I realize, that I never thought I'd hear, not in this context, and not from a man. Words that, right now, I desperately need to hear.

My head says it's too soon to say this. But in my heart? It feels right. It feels true. And I can't stop the reply rolling off my lips.

"I love you too, Russell."

shots

Russell and I sit around a table with his friends. We're playing poker, and anytime someone loses a hand, they have to take a shot of whiskey. This is my first time playing poker, and I don't know what I'm doing with the cards. Before long, my head is swimming. I fold, saying, "I need to sit the next few rounds out."

"The baby is tired," says Reynolds.

"I'm not a baby," I say.

"You're Russell's baby," Reynolds says. "He's robbing the cradle."

Russell laughs along with his friends. "He's not a child," Russell defends himself. "He's a young man."

"Emphasis on young," Kyle says.

Turner shuffles the deck, then deals. I excuse myself to the kitchen and get a glass of water. When I come back, they're all deep in the game.

Reynolds wins the next hand. Russell, Kyle, and Turner

each take a shot of Jack Daniel's. Russell doesn't seem to mind, though. Even though he's losing nearly every hand, he's laughing and smiling, and winking at me from across the room.

I'm on the couch asleep when they wrap up the game. I wake and look at the clock, and it's just past midnight. "Come on, Sexy Rexy. Time to go home," Russell slurs. He trips and half falls over the coffee table, barely catching himself before his head slams into it.

"Someone lost hard tonight," Reynolds says. He claps Russell on the back. "Win some, lose some. Or, in your case, lose some, lose 'em all."

Russell rolls his eyes. He fishes the keys out of his pocket, looks at me, and motions his head toward the door. "Let's roll."

"I sobered up. Why don't I drive us home?"

"I can drive," Russell slurs.

"I think you might be a little drunk," I say. "I don't mind driving."

" 'S my Jeep, my rules."

"I'm with the child bride on this one," Reynolds says, snatching the keys from Russell and handing them to me.

Russell lunges at me and tries to wrestle the keys out of my hand. "No. I can drive."

"You really can't," Reynolds says. He walks us out, making sure Russell sits in the passenger seat. He buckles him in. Looks at me, saying, "Get home safely."

As soon as I start the engine, Russell slurs, "Lemme drive."

"It's fine. I got it."

"I can drive. I'm not drunk."

"I know," I say, "but I really think I should drive. Please."

"Whatever," Russell says, crossing his arms.

Halfway home, Russell says, "Pull over."

"Are you gonna be sick?"

"Pull over," he repeats.

I pull the Jeep onto the side of the road. Russell opens his door, comes around, and opens the driver's door. "Get out. Lemme drive."

"Russell. You can't."

"I can do whatever I want," he slurs. He tries to pull me out of the driver's seat. He grabs my neck. He snaps, "Move it, faggot."

"What'd you call me?"

"You heard me."

"Get back in your seat," I say. "I'm trying to get you home safely."

" 'S my Jeep," he says. "You don't like it, you can walk home."

"Are you fucking serious?"

"Dead serious."

"Fine." I unbuckle my seat belt and get out. I start walking. I'm fuming.

A few minutes later, Russell's Jeep swerves to my side, nearly hitting me. He shouts out the window, "Get in."

"No."

"I said, get in," he growls. "You hear me? Get in the fucking Jeep."

"Fuck, no. I don't get in cars with drunks."

"You think I'm a drunk?"

"You are right now."

"Goddammit, get in the fucking car, Rex."

"No."

"Fuck you, then," he says. The Jeep peels out. It barely

misses a pole as Russell swerves around the next corner well over the speed limit.

I walk back to Russell's in the dark.

———

When I get home half an hour later, Russell is on the couch, crying. "I'm sorry. I didn't mean it."

"Yeah, I'm pretty sure you did."

"I didn't. I swear. You know I love you." He gets up, wrapping his arms around me. I don't hug him back. He whispers in my ear, "I love you. I love you. I love you."

"You were being an asshole."

"I'm pig-head stubborn. I know that. I'm sorry—please forgive me."

"I'll forgive you tomorrow."

"No, come on, baby. Don't be like that."

"Don't call me baby."

"Rex, please. Say you love me." He's holding my arms, squeezing them. "Come on, just say it."

"Russell, let go."

"Say you love me."

"I do. Just let me go."

Russell lets go. I walk into the bathroom and close the door. I brush my teeth, then piss. After I flush, I hear Russell is crying again. I want to go to bed, but Russell is sitting on the foot of it, his face in his palms. "I'm sorry, okay? Don't be mad at me. I never want to hurt you. Please say you'll forgive me. Say you love me."

Annoyed, I take a deep breath. I go to the kitchen and get him a glass of water. I come back. "Drink this."

He holds the glass, but just stares at the water. "I don't know why I'm like this. I just love you so much. And I'm scared you're going to leave me."

I think, And go where?

Just thinking that makes my heart sink.

I love Russell, but I don't want to feel trapped with him by circumstance. I want to be here cause I want to be here. Cause I have a choice.

"Rex, please." Russell pats the bed next to him until I sit. "I've never met anyone like you. I fell for you as soon as I saw you. I love you. I love you so much, it hurts."

If he were sober and saying this, I think it'd fill me with warmth. But right now, in this moment, him drunk and slurring, it rubs me the wrong way. Like he just needs someone to say they love him. Like I might be replaceable.

"I love you," he says again.

"I know," I say.

"Say it back to me."

"I don't feel like it."

"Say it," he says, tears in his eyes. "I need to hear you say it."

I don't want to. But I say it anyway. "I love you."

He leans over, trying to kiss me. I let him. His hand rubs my leg, moves up to my crotch, groping me . . . until I push his hand away. "I'm not in the mood."

"Come on," he says, kissing my neck, trying to push me onto my back. "I love you. I love you so much."

"Russell, I said I wasn't in the mood."

"Well, get in the mood!" he snaps.

I stand up. "No."

"No? No?" he growls. "Listen up, you little shit. If you wanna stay here, you better put out."

It's like he's just punched me in the stomach. All the breath goes out of me.

Suddenly I want to leave. If I had a place to go to, I would. Right fucking now. But I don't. And he knows that. He has the upper hand. He has a full house, and I have no hand to play. I'm in a losing position. And there's no one to deal another hand.

"I'm sleeping in my truck," I say.

"Good," he says. "Enjoy the night air."

I storm out, slamming the door.

In the bed of my truck, I lie on my back, staring up at the overcast sky, wishing I could see the stars.

————

The next morning, I wake with a crick in my neck. I'm all sore from sleeping on the metal bed of my truck. When I finally go inside, Russell is on the futon, visibly upset. "Where have you been?"

"I slept in my truck."

"What? Why?" His eyes are beyond confused. They're bewildered.

"Cause of last night."

"What happened?" he asks, and already his eyes are full of remorse.

"You don't remember?"

"I must've blacked out," he says. "Last thing I remember is playing cards at Reynolds's place."

"Yeah, well, you turned into a real prick on the way home."

Russell's eyes well up with tears. "What did I do?"

I look around at the ceiling. I don't want to rehash it. I don't want to fight. I don't want to feel powerless. Like I have no control here. But I don't.

All I say is, "You were cruel."

Russell starts crying. "Shit. Shit shit shit." He punches his own head. "I'm sorry, Rex. I don't know what I said or did, but you have to know I didn't mean it. I love you."

His face falls into his palms as he starts to sob. "Don't leave me, Rex. I don't know what I'd do without you. I'm sorry. I'm so, so sorry. Please forgive me." Not realizing he said the same thing last night.

But this time, this time, I feel like he means it. He's sober. His eyes are full of tears. And everything about him is the Russell I know. The Russell I fell for.

I sit down next to him. He hugs me.

"I love you. I never want to hurt you. Please don't leave me. I need you. Promise me you'll stay. I love you."

Then I'm crying too. Cause I feel needed. Like I have a place here. He wants me here. He wants me for me. Me.

Then he's kissing me. Our wet cheeks press together. He kisses me over and over, in between repeating himself. "I love you." Kiss. "Please don't leave me." Kiss. "You have to promise me you'll stay." Kiss.

Then he starts taking my clothes off, still saying, "I love you. I love you so much. It won't happen again. I swear."

I want to believe him. I really do.

So why don't I?

college

I still haven't heard back about a job. Any job.

But I've been thinking, maybe I should skip to the last part of my plan. Get into college and get my life on track again.

On Monday, I walk to Tulane and Loyola. The two private universities are practically next to each other. They both have tree-lined sidewalks. Students my age mill about. They sit on metal benches, headphones over their ears. They skateboard or throw footballs to one another. Or they lie on the grass, studying with friends and having picnics. This is what I should be doing.

At each admissions office, I inquire about enrollment, scholarships, and tuition. The cost alone is well over anything I can afford. Even if I received financial aid, I don't have the money for the application fees that I need now. And if I did, I'd still have to wait until the winter semester. I can't start in the fall. So it'd be six months of what? Waiting around? Sitting on Russell's futon? Biding my time before my life begins again?

I walk back to Russell's place, then pace until my legs are

tired. I glance at the futon every few steps. I don't want to sit down. I want to do something. I want to fix everything. I don't want to give up. But I sit. I stare at the wall, trying to figure out what I can do. After four hours, I still have no idea. An ache rocks through me as the pit in my stomach grows heavier.

———

On Tuesday, I drive to the University of New Orleans.

The woman in the admissions office wears her brown hair in a tight bun. She smiles. But her face falls as I explain my situation. I fell out with my family. I'm staying with a friend. I made straight A's in high school. I took almost all honors and advanced placement classes. I scored a 1480 on my SATs. But now I need to start my college career.

"I'm so sorry for your situation. The good news is it sounds like you're a wonderful candidate for our school. We can waive the application fee if you fill out a hardship form. But you'll have to pay out-of-state tuition until you've lived in Louisiana for at least two years."

"But I can take out loans? I could start in September?"

"I'm afraid you missed the deadline for financial aid, and for the fall semester. But we could help you be ready in time for January."

"You don't understand," I say. "I have to get into college as soon as possible. I need to move into the dorms. I need to get a loan so I can feed myself."

"I'm sorry," she says. "But my hands are tied."

I'm lost somewhere between anger and tears. I want to punch something. I want to punch the universe in the face for putting me in this situation. I want to punch my dad in the face for putting me in this position. And I want to punch myself in the face, for finding myself here, helpless. Powerless. Trapped by too many conditions out of my control.

"Keep up your fortitude. With your attitude and conviction, you'll make a fine student anywhere. Please. Take these forms home, fill them out, and I'll help you make it in for the spring semester."

January is a lifetime away. I can't wait that long. But what choice do I have?

I exit the admissions office, my head hung low. My hands are full of brochures and flyers and applications, but there's a lot less hope in my heart.

family

I'm in the shower, eyes closed, washing my hair, when a hand lands on my back. Startled, I scream.

Russell starts laughing. Naked, he steps into the shower behind me. "Your face, dude. That was hilarious."

"I'll get you back," I say.

"Well, let me get your back," he says. He picks up the soap and starts massaging my back with it. "So what are you doing this weekend?"

I try not to laugh. "Oh, well, sorry. I have a packed schedule."

"Oh? Doing what?"

"You know, this and that. Watching sports, hanging with friends, getting drunk on Bourbon Street, probably going to find me a date with a hot man . . ."

"You better not be dating anybody else," Russell says. He turns me around, kisses me. I kiss him back. Then he bends down, rests on his knees while he soaps my thighs, my calves, and then my feet. When his fingers slide between my toes, I start laughing.

"That tickles."

"Good," he says, smiling up at me. As bad as everything is, Russell is the one source of light in my life.

When he's not drunk.

"This weekend," Russell says, "I want you to meet my family."

"For real?"

"These past few weeks, getting to know you, I feel so close to you. I love you. Some people might think we're moving too fast, but I feel it in my gut. This is right. And my family is important to me. So I want you to meet them. They're having a good ole-fashioned barbeque Saturday. What'dya say? Wanna be my date?"

"Yeah," I say. "Yeah, I'd like that."

———

It takes a little under two hours to drive to the small town of Belle Rose. My palms are sweating more the closer we get. Russell takes my hand and kisses the back of it. "Nothing to be nervous about."

"I want them to like me."

"Then just be yourself," Russell says. He squeezes my hand.

His rural hometown stretches out. We pass an old movie theater, a church, a post office, a library, another church, long swaths of land between each one. Russell points out where he went to school, where he played football, where he came out to his cousin. Finally, we turn down a driveway leading to a modest house.

It's bigger than any of the apartments I grew up in with my mom, but smaller than my dad's house. It has none of the personality of the buildings in New Orleans, but it's charming, it feels like a home for a family.

"This is where you grew up with three brothers and two sisters?"

"Yup. Boys in one room, girls in the other," he says.

Once we're out of the Jeep, I can already hear a cacophony of voices from the backyard. Turning the corner, we're greeted by the hoots and hollers of a dozen people. Russell's mom wears a striped dress and has soft features. She rushes over and grabs Russell's face, kissing her son on both of his cheeks. Then she turns to me. "You must be Rex."

I stick out my hand. "Nice to meet you, Mrs. Dawes."

"Mrs. Dawes is my mother-in-law. You call me Mama." She embraces me, hugs me in close. The soft scents of lilac and rose stir my nose.

Russell introduces me to his father. For some reason, I expected a gruff old man. Instead, he's cheerful, round, with a beer in one hand and a cigar in the other. He plops the stogie in his mouth and pats me on the back. "Welcome, welcome. Get yourself a drink."

I'm tempted to drink a beer to settle my nerves, but the last thing I want is to drink too much and make a fool of myself. Instead, I pour myself a soda.

Russell spends the next five minutes hugging and wrestling with his horde of nieces and nephews. When he points at me, he says, "Say hi to my boyfriend."

He says it so casually, it makes me reel. It's the first time he's called me that. More than that, I can't imagine saying, "This is my boyfriend," to anyone, let alone my family. It's so alien, it feels like an actual alien walking out into the crowd would be less strange.

The kids swarm around me, saying, "Hi," and "Hello," and

"How old are you?" The youngest girl offers me a Barbie doll to play with. After Russell introduces me to each of them, he moves to present me to their parents.

"This is my brother, Michael, his wife, Lonnie. My sister, Dawn, my other brother, Keith, and his wife, Charlaine. And this is my cousin, Dana . . ."

Dana waves over another woman, with long brown hair. "This is my wife, Kelly."

"You're . . ." I begin.

Dana finishes for me. "Gay? Yup. Russell didn't tell you?"

Russell smiles at me. "I'm gay. Dana's gay. Brad's gay. Val is gay. Tyson is gay."

"Uncle Frank is gay," Dana adds. She elbows Russell. "You realize it's always the third one born in each family unit."

"Yup. And folks say it's not genetic."

"Seriously?" I ask. "You have that many gay people in your family?"

Russell and Dana nod.

"Who cares about who's gay? I'm hungry," Michael calls out. "Come on, let's eat already, folks."

A large picnic table leans against the house. Russell pulls me into line behind his brother and his kids, and hands me a paper plate. The table is overflowing with food and drink. A variety of two-liter bottles of soda stand next to three bags of Lay's potato chips, each with its own flavor. BBQ, Sour Cream & Onion, and Original. Russell's mom cuts the line to remove foil from the aluminum trays. Steam rises up from corn on the cob, grits, and collard greens. There's a tray of crawfish, and another of light gray sausage that makes me recoil.

"What is that?" I whisper to Russell.

"You ain't ever had boudin before? You gotta try it." He picks up a link, takes a bite, and drops the rest on my plate. I've never been a fan of sausage, and the gray makes me even more cautious. I want to be polite. So I agree to try it.

I take a small bite. As I chew, chunks of gristle and fat roll around in my mouth, making me want to gag. Forcing myself to swallow, I toss the boudin back on Russell's plate. "Thanks but no thanks."

When we're sitting down, Russell's family starts talking about an upcoming church function. All I can concentrate on is the food, though. I'm trying desperately to get my plastic fork to break up a crawfish's shelled backside.

Russell watches me for a minute, then laughs. "Haven't you ever eaten crawfish before?"

"I had lobster once."

"Doesn't count." Russell picks up a crawfish from his plate. "First, you hold it on either side of the tail. Twist and snap the head away. Then you suck out the yellow stuff from the head." Russell slurps it down.

"Oh my god. Is that shellfish brains?"

Russell shrugs. "I don't know, but it's mighty tasty." He tosses the head into a pail where everyone is discarding their heads. "Now you peel the shell away, just like shrimp. Then you tug the tail meat out, and dip it in butter."

After a couple tries, I finally get the hang of it. It's not bad. I'm not sure if I actually like the crawfish meat, or if I just like the butter.

But I eat until I'm stuffed. Russell pats his belly. "Thanks, Mama. Always good eating with you around."

"Hope you saved room," she says. "I made some old-fashioned Cajun cake." She brings the dessert to the table and carves out

a hefty slice, plopping it down in front of me. The pineapple-
and-pecan cake is topped with coconut and more pecans. It's
so good, I have to ask for a second slice after everyone else has
gotten their fill.

By that time, the sun has gone down and the family is sitting
around a fire, drinking beer. ". . . then there was that time
Russell pulled off his diaper, full of more poo than his little body
shoulda been able to make, and slung it across the living room
wall, smearing shit all over the dang place," Michael shares.

We're all laughing, even Russell, whose saying, "Well, now,
I don't remember that."

"Oh, it happened," his brother says.

"That it did," Russell's dad agrees.

"You remember?" Russell asks.

"Who do you think had to clean it up?"

"How about you, Rex?" Michael asks. "Your dad ever have
to clean your shit off the wall?"

I'm caught off guard. The mention of my dad freezes me
like a deer in headlights. I'm not sure what to say, but Russell
steps in. "Let's not talk about Rex's dad."

"Oh shit. I'm sorry," Michael says. "I forgot."

My face flushes red as I look to Russell. "You told them?"

"I told Mama," Russell says.

"And I told the rest," Mama says, "not to gossip, but to
share, hoping they'd be polite and mind their manners and not
bring it up. Nothing for you to be ashamed of."

"But it's embarrassing."

"Not for you, it's not," Mama says. She walks over, hugs me
from behind, and whispers, "The only one who should feel bad
is your daddy."

three

At Reynolds's apartment, the three of us are watching *The Mask* on TV. Jim Carrey is donning a green face and acting a fool. Russell is curled up next to me with a glass of wine in his hand. He nestles his head on my shoulder, but I notice his foot rubbing up against Reynolds's leg. A pang of jealousy spins through me.

I catch myself. It's nothing. An accident. They're friends. They have been for a lot longer than I've known Russell.

After the movie, Reynolds hops up. From his kitchenette, he waves two wine bottles, both empty of red. He pulls the foil cap off a third bottle and twists the corkscrew in. "Who's ready for another glass?"

Russell chugs what's left in his glass and waves it in the air. "Yes, please."

"I'm good," I say.

"Don't be silly," Reynolds says. He pours, refilling my glass.

This is my fourth one, and I'm starting to feel like I'm floating. "Wine is heart-healthy. And good for the ole noggin."

I say, "We have to drive home, though."

"You can both crash here. I have plenty of room," Reynolds says. "It'll be an old-fashioned slumber party."

"I forgot my pajamas," Russell says.

"Guess you'll have to sleep naked." Reynolds smirks at Russell, who grins back.

After the movie, Reynolds turns off the TV and puts an Enya CD in the player. The calm chanting fills the room with soft melody as he dims the lights. When he comes back, he plops onto the couch with a little hop. He sits next to me instead of Russell, so I'm in the middle between the two of them.

"So how's it going, Sexy Rexy?" Reynolds says. "You enjoying the Big Easy?"

"The Big Easy?"

"It's another name for our fair city," he says, "cause everything here is easy."

"You're easy," Russell says.

Reynolds smacks Russell with a couch pillow, almost spilling our glasses of wine.

I say, "Yeah, I like it here."

Reynolds takes a large sip from his glass. His head swivels from me to Russell. "So who's the top and who's the bottom?"

I almost spit out the wine I was drinking. Instead, I swallow it down, choking on it when it starts going down the wrong hatch.

Reynolds pats my back. "I didn't realize you were so delicate, baby boy."

"I'm not delicate."

"I'm a top," Russell says, "as you well know."

"How does Reynolds know?" I ask.

"Russell didn't tell you?" Reynolds says with a snicker. "We used to date."

"You did?"

"Ages ago," Russell says. "Long before I met you."

"And I was the top," Reynolds says.

"No, you weren't, you big bottom," Russell argues.

"As I recall, we both took turns. Now quit dodging my question." Reynolds looks at me with eyes like a hungry crocodile's. "Well, Rex, are you giving or taking?"

My face reddens. I'm not used to talking about gay sex.

Russell throws his hands up. "Fine. So, yeah, I'm bottoming for him. But look at this face . . ." He reaches over and squeezes my cheeks. "How can I say no to that?" He kisses me on the lips.

Reynolds's smile irritates me. "Kiss for me again."

Russell leans over and starts kissing me. I reluctantly return the kiss. But when I feel Reynolds staring, I pull back.

"Hot." Reynolds adds, "You're a good kisser, Rex. I can tell."

"Thanks," I say awkwardly. I look from one of them to the other, feeling some kind of tension. Suddenly our age differences seem more apparent. Russell more than a decade older than me, and Reynolds a decade on top of that. Twenty years between me and Reynolds. He could be my dad. And the way he's leering at me . . .

It bothers me.

Reynolds finishes off his glass of wine in one gulp, then pours another. He refills Russell's glass and tops off mine, even though I've only had a sip.

"So, Rex, what do you like to do?"

"Um . . . swimming, biking, reading, mostly—comics books, sci-fi and fantasy novels, Anne Rice, stuff like that."

Russell and Reynolds both laugh, exchanging a mischievous glance. "That's *not* what I meant," Reynolds says.

"He means what do you like *in bed*," Russell explains.

"Oh, um. The usual stuff. I guess."

Reynolds raises his eyebrows, leaning toward me. "Like what?"

Shifting in my seat, I place my wineglass on the coffee table and lean toward Russell. "It's getting late. Maybe we should get going."

"I've had too much to drink," Russell says. "Let's just crash here."

"You two can sleep in my bed," Reynolds says.

"Where are you going to sleep?"

Reynolds's lips curl up, and he takes a long sip from his glass of wine. "We'll figure it out." Russell and Reynolds clink their glasses together, eyes locked. Like they're having some kind of conversation in silence, one that I don't understand. Except that I get the gist.

And I don't want to.

"I can drive," I say to Russell.

"You've had four glasses of wine. And I know how you are about not drinking-and-driving," Russell says. "Am I right?"

Nauseous, I nod. I shouldn't have drunk so much. But Reynolds kept pouring. And I didn't think anything of it. I didn't realize there was some plan in motion.

"Yeah, just stay here," Reynolds says. He puts his hand on

my knee. He traces a finger up my leg to the hem of my shorts. A chill runs through me. "You're getting goose bumps."

I stand up suddenly, nearly knocking over the wine on the coffee table. "I don't feel so well."

"What do you mean?" Russell asks.

"I don't know. It's my stomach," I say. "I think you're right. I drank too much. I think, um, maybe we should just go to sleep."

"I'm not tired," Russell says, annoyance in his voice. "Come here. Lie down between us, and we'll rub your stomach."

"I'm good," I say.

"Why don't you go lie down in my bed?" Reynolds says.

I peer down the dark hall into the darker bedroom. I really don't feel well. There aren't butterflies in my stomach, but agitated roaches. Thousands of them.

"Okay," I say.

"Do you need a tuck-in?" Reynolds asks. Russell's smile matches his friend's.

"No, thanks."

"Your loss." Reynolds winks at me.

I don't know why, but I say, "You two have fun."

"Oh, we will," Russell says.

I walk down the hallway and enter the dark room. I close the door behind me. I have to resist the urge to lock it.

I don't take anything off. My shorts, my shirt, my socks, they all stay on. I crawl into the tall bed, on top of the sheets, and pull the comforter over me. I listen for a long time to hushed whispers, catching a phrase here and there: " . . . not old enough . . ." " . . . doesn't know what he's missing . . ." " . . . when he's older . . ."

I hear the TV come back on, and I'm comforted by it. After a while, I drift off to sleep. Then I'm woken by the soft grunts and moans drifting in from under the door.

I don't know what's happening out there.

And I don't want to.

So I pretend it's nothing. It's just the TV.

crabs

When Russell comes home from work, he doesn't kiss me like he usually does. He seems sheepish. I ask, "What's wrong?"

"Nothing," he says. Then he disappears into the bathroom for the next half hour. When he comes out, he says, "We might have a problem."

"What problem?"

He can't look me in the eyes as his face reddens. "I think we have crabs."

"Crabs?" I think of the little pink crustaceans that skitter across the beach on eight legs, raising their little claws. I almost giggle. "You mean for dinner."

Russell points down to his crotch. "Crabs."

"I'm so confused," I say.

"Pubic lice," he says. "Reynolds has them, and I think we picked them up when we spent the night."

I ask, "How do you get crabs?"

"You can pick them up from clothes and bedding," he says.
"And sex?"

Russell shakes his head. "Yeah, but that's not what happened."

"You sure?" I growl, feeling anger rising up in my throat.

Russell's glare is biting. "I didn't cheat on you. If anything,
you're probably cheating on me all day while I'm at work."

"I haven't cheated on you. I haven't even made any friends,"
I yell in my defense. "All I do is look for jobs!"

"And watch TV," Russell shouts, "while I'm out working all
day. I'm the one paying all the bills. You think it's cheap taking
care of another person?"

None of that is untrue. So my anger melts into shame.
Humiliation washes over me, all my failed attempts at securing
anything in the way of employment. Feeling sick to my stomach,
I look down at the floor.

Russell stands over me, sneering, "Got nothing to say now?"

I can't say anything.

What right do I have?

I don't know why, but I say, "I'm sorry."

Russell goes to the kitchen and leans against the counter.
After a minute, he sighs. "Sorry I snapped at you. I've just been
really stressed. Money and stuff. Doesn't help that I've been
itching like crazy."

"From what?"

"I don't know. The crabs, maybe?"

"Oh." I try to forget the last few minutes and focus on the
problem at hand. "How do we get rid of them?"

Russell seems to relax. "First we have to check and see if we
got them. Come on." He leads me into the bathroom and says,
"Get naked."

I take off my shirt and drop my shorts. Russell gets on his knees and pulls down my boxers. Usually this leads to something else. Instead, Russell starts prying through my pubic hair. I snort, nearly bursting into laughter.

"What?" Russell says.

"Ever see those *National Geographic* nature documentaries? The ones where the monkeys groom one another, then eat whatever little insects they find? This feels like that."

Russell snorts, then laughs too.

He makes a monkey sound. Then we're both laughing.

His fingers return to inspecting, and it's tickling me. I keep giggling, and so does he. Finally, he says. "Hmm. I didn't find any. Guess you're clean."

Relief washes over me.

"My turn," Russell says. He pulls off his shirt and undoes his belt. His pants fall around his ankles. I tug off his underwear. Now I can't stop laughing.

My fingers wander through his pubes, inch by inch, like a detective searching out clues with a magnifying glass.

I say, "I don't see anything."

"Good," he says. "But after this, we should wash all the bedding and all our clothes in hot water. Just in case."

"And if we do have them?"

"Then we need to shave every inch of hair from our neck down."

"Are you serious? We'd look like dolphins!"

"Like little babies."

"Babies with crabs."

"That's why you have to shave. To get rid of them and their nits."

"Nits?"

"Lice eggs."

I shiver all over, almost gagging at the thought of an infestation. I spend the next twenty minutes searching every inch of Russell's crotch, his leg hair, and even the peach fuzz on his ass cheeks. "That's it. I didn't find any."

Russell lets out a heavy sigh. "Thank god. Crabs are the worst."

no

Russell and I go to dinner around the corner from his place. In between the spicy jalapeño cornbread appetizer and the main course of red beans and rice, we manage to put away two bottles of wine. We're both tipsy on the walk back to Russell's.

He throws his arm around my neck and starts singing Garth Brooks at me. I don't know the song, but it's clearly a song about love. I try not to laugh at Russell's crooning when it's so heartfelt. When we get home, Russell fumbles the keys, and I have to help him recover them. Inside, he opens another bottle of wine.

"No, no, no," I slur. "We've had enough."

"Just one more glass," he says.

"We're going to be so hungover tomorrow."

"Live in the moment," he garbles.

He pours two glasses, insistent that I take the second. I take the tiniest of sips as we drink on the couch. Russell stumbles through stories of ex-boyfriends, explaining he's always been the man, the top in his relationships. Until me. I know that's not entirely true cause of Reynolds.

Then Russell asks, "When are you going to bottom for me?"

"Um . . . that's not really my thing."

Russell glares. "What if I'm tired of bottoming?"

"You're not. You enjoy it way too much." I try to kiss him, but he pushes me away.

"Yeah, well, I wanna fuck you," he says. "I deserve that much. I'm the man in the relationship. I work all day, I pay for everything. That dinner you just ate? That wine you just drank? The electricity that pays for you to sit around all day in the air-conditioning watching TV? You need to show some respect."

"I do respect you," I say slowly. "And I'm grateful. Honestly, I am. But that doesn't mean I want to take it like that."

"What's your problem?"

"It'll hurt," I say.

"Not if you do it right."

"Yeah, well, I'm not eager to try," I say. Then I add, "Look, I just don't want to, okay?"

Russell rolls his eyes. We sit there in silence. Russell finishes his wine, some escaping, dripping down his chin. He hits his chest. "You owe me."

"I don't owe you anything," I growl. But already I don't believe my own words. And he can tell just by looking at me.

He crosses his arms, pouting. "Yeah, well, let me know when you're ready to put out. I'm not going to wait forever." He stumbles to his feet and storms off to bed. I wait until I hear him snoring to crawl into the bed myself. I don't try to cuddle with him. I go to sleep at the edge on my side of his bed.

———

I'm passed out when Russell pulls my boxers off. He rolls me onto my stomach. As I start to come to, he's on top of me. Trying to shove himself inside of me.

"Russell, stop," I say. I move to get out from under him, my arms pushing. But his elbow presses down on the back of my neck, while his other hand holds mine down. I'm stammering, "Get off me."

"Shhhh," he says. "Just relax."

"You're hurting me."

"That's because you're moving."

"Russell!"

"Shhhh. Come on. You'll like it. Trust me."

"No."

"Shut up. You owe me this," he growls in my ear.

"No! Stop!" I wail, struggling beneath him. "Get off me. I said no."

I'm trying to get up, kicking, pushing with my arms, but he's bigger than me. Heavier. Stronger. He keeps going. Pushing. Thrusting. Grunting.

I'm trying not to cry. But I can't help it. It hurts. My tears drop onto the pillow.

"Relax," he says. "Just relax."

The more I struggle, the weaker I get. I'm too drunk, my limbs too slow. Still, I'm working to get out from under him. Trying to escape.

"Russell, stop. Please."

He pushes my face into the mattress, saying, "Shhh. It's okay."

The more I cry, the more I say no, the more I beg him to

stop, the harder he goes. My strength starts to fail me. And I hear my voice getting smaller. Quieter. Shrinking away from me.

Maybe cause I do owe him. Cause he owns me in some way. Cause he's been taking care of me when no one else would. Cause on some level, I feel like nothing. Worthless. Less than human. Rejected by society for being different. Discarded by my father. Like an old shoe that no longer fits. Like unwanted furniture.

Then I'm outside my body. Above myself. Above Russell. Watching him on top of me. And I see myself struggling.

Then struggling less.

And less.

Until I'm not.

Until I give in.

Until I give up.

And let it happen.

leaving

The next morning, after Russell goes to work, I pack. My books and toiletries go back into my backpack. My clothes back into my duffel bag. I drop the spare key in the bowl on the kitchen counter . . .

And leave.

what I have

The radio plays on my truck radio, but I can't hear the songs. I'm too busy trying to breathe. What am I doing? Why am I leaving Russell's? Where am I going to live? How am I going to eat? When is this sick feeling growing in my body going to go away?

Deep breaths.

I try to think of what I have.

My truck.

A quarter tank of gas.

The clothes on my body:

Underwear, socks, jean shorts, a T-shirt, a ball cap, shoes.

My backpack, which contains:

A toothbrush. Toothpaste. Deodorant. A few paperback books.

My duffel bag, which contains:

Underwear, socks, shorts, a pair of jeans, shirts, a sweatshirt, a hoodie.

My wallet, which contains:

My Social Security card, my driver's license, a video rental card, the book page scribbled with Russell's phone number . . . I pull the truck over, rip the paper out of my wallet, crumple it in my hand, and throw it out the window.

Inside my wallet, I have twenty-two dollars.

There's also some change in my pocket.

I don't know what the fuck I'm going to do.

driving

Without a destination in mind, I drive.

But I want to jump out of my skin.

My chest is so tight it might explode. Instead, I start screaming. I pound my fists down, hitting the steering wheel again and again and again. Until I'm weeping.

Why did Russell do that? Why did he ruin everything?

When I wipe my tears with the back of my arm, I smell Russell on me. His musk triggers a race of memories. All the good. Then all the bad. And last night.

My stomach flips upside down. I pull the truck over, opening the door just in time to throw up. When I'm done, I wipe my mouth and sit back. My anus throbs, it's excruciating just to move. And I'm crying all over again.

My dad gave me a choice. And I left.

Then, whether he intended to or not, Russell gave me a choice. And I left.

Both times, I hesitated. Torn. Comfort and security and what I know, versus pure uncertainty.

Both times, I made the decision. I had to leave. Even though I have next to nothing, I still have control over my own body, over my future.

But is that enough? Do I have control over my future now?

I slap myself, trying to get out of my head. To stop feeling sorry for myself. "Pull it together, Rex," I whisper. I tell myself what I've told myself for years: "You'll be fine. You're like a cat. You have nine lives. You'll land on your feet."

I sniff, swallowing back snot. I need to focus on the next steps. What now?

I need a job if I'm going to take care of myself.

So I drive down all the main streets, looking at all the places I applied for jobs. I park a few blocks over in the residential area, where there's no meters to pay. Then I walk from restaurant to restaurant and from store to store, checking on my applications.

"I'm sorry, we're fully staffed."

"We're not hiring right now, but we'll call you."

"Unfortunately, it looks like you don't have enough experience."

Are they sorry, though? And how are they going to contact me without me having access to Russell's phone and answering machine? And am I really too underqualified to serve coffee? Or can they tell something is wrong with me? My red eyes, my puffy cheeks, my tired walk. That under the surface I'm desperate.

As I trudge back to my truck, the sun's rays fall on my skin. The sky bears down on my shoulders. Sweat drips down my spine, into my shorts, into my boxers. It's hard to breathe in this oppressive heat. And the weight of the world presses me further and further down as questions swirl through my head. The same questions I was asking myself when I first got to New Orleans. Like the last few weeks never happened.

Why is this happening to me? What did I do to deserve this? It's like pain was planted in me, and now it's growing uncontrollably.

I ask myself again, What do I do now?

Part of me wonders if I should just go back to Russell's. I could unpack. Put my stuff back where it was. Maybe he'd come home and apologize. He'd never know that I was going to leave. Maybe last night was a mistake. After all, he was drunk.

But no. I left the keys, letting the door lock itself behind me. Like some part of my subconscious knew I might second-guess myself. Like I might try to undo my decision. Like it wanted to remind me why I left.

I don't want to take anything else from him.

hum

Under the buzz of the fluorescent lights, aisles and aisles of food spread out before me. Boxes and jars and packs of pasta and jellies and chips. Fresh fruits and produce, ice cream and milk, cakes and baked goods. So much food I shouldn't buy.

Cause I already know I have to budget to make my cash last.

I want to leave the grocery store. But the sun has long set, and I can't fight off my hunger any longer. I have to find something to eat. Something cheap.

I come across a four-unit package of ramen noodles. I have no idea where I'd find boiling water to simmer the curvy dry pasta into life. And it's so hot out. Do I really want hot soup? I would if it were an option. I consider cereal, but have no idea where I'd store the milk. It would spoil outside a fridge. It wouldn't last.

This late at night, the store is mostly empty. I look around for mirrors or cameras. I think how easy it would be to put something in my backpack. To slip in sticks of beef jerky or a bag of chips. But the last thing I need is to get arrested. To go to jail for shoplifting. I'm hungry, but I'm not that hungry.

Finally, I settle on a jar of peanut butter, the cheapest one they have. A loaf of bread, the cheapest one they have. A hand of bananas. And a gallon of water, the cheapest one they have. It isn't much, but it should last me a few days if I stretch it.

There's only one cashier. Two people wait in front of me with their carts full to overflowing. My stomach aches, and I want to eat one of the bananas in line. But I force myself to wait.

The hum of the store air conditioner reminds me of Russell's window unit. Of the quiet hum of his air conditioner. Of his own soft purring while he slept. Of cuddling up next to him. Of feeling loved.

My thoughts are betraying me, and I can't stop them.

When it's finally my turn to check out, the cashier doesn't even look at me. She scans my items, each with a digital *beep*. She puts everything in one thin plastic grocery bag. I pay. As I hand her the dollar bills and the change, I want to cry again.

I walk out into the dark parking lot and make my way to my truck. In the driver's seat, I open my bag and take out one banana. I eat it slowly, trying to make it last. I need to pace my eating. I need to watch every morsel of food I have now.

My mind goes back to Russell.

Why didn't I stay?

I could've gotten a job at any moment. My college application to the University of New Orleans was all filled out. The essays were written. The hardship form explained why I needed the school to cover my fees. All I had to do was turn it all in.

But the forms had Russell's address and phone number on them. Could I really have stayed for six more months? Maybe last night was a fluke. A misunderstanding. Maybe he's at home right now, having found me gone, crying. Regretting what he'd done.

Maybe if I give him another chance . . .

But am I missing him? Or missing the security of his home?

His TV. His futon. His air conditioner. His fridge. His shower. A yellow rubber duck, smiling, sitting on the back of his toilet. They were all comforting. But as I recall his house, I recall the bed—the bed that I could see from the living room through the shotgun doorway. If I stayed, it would stare back at me. Reminding me.

And Russell?

I think of our meeting in the ocean. I think of that Pensacola hotel. I think of our kiss. Of our first date. Of the first time we had sex. Of him holding me at night. And me holding him. Of him saying he loved me. And me returning the sentiment. And meaning it.

I did mean it. I do miss him. I miss him so much it hurts.

I never thought he would hurt me like that.

But he did.

Even after I said no.

He took what he wanted.

So why does some part of me miss him? What does that say about me?

If I'm honest, I miss my dad too.

And my mom and stepdad.

I miss everyone who hurt me.

I miss my old life.

But it's in the past. It's already gone. And I can never get it back.

seatbelt

I drive down a street of houses, all unfamiliar to me.

An open space sits between a truck and a four-door car. I pull up alongside the car, then reverse, parallel-parking underneath a tree.

I move the stick shift into first and turn off the ignition.

Homes on either side of the street seem to watch me, their windows becoming eyes, their doors becoming mouths. But all of the doors are closed to me. Envy rolls through me when I think of the beds inside.

I'm so tired. I barely slept last night, after . . .

I don't want to think about that.

Like the first night I was in New Orleans, I lie down on my bucket seat, curling into the shape of an armadillo. I prop my duffel bag under my head as a pillow, then adjust my legs so they aren't crushed against the steering wheel. Once again, the seat belt buckle stabs into my back. I try to angle myself to avoid it.

As I approach sleep, my body makes the slightest jerk. This

causes the buckle to poke, knifing at my spine. So I turn over, facing the other direction, but my whole backside is hanging off the seats, gravity threatening to pull me onto the floor. And now the stick shift is prodding my back. I change positions again and again.

I can't get comfortable.

But even if I could, I would still be crying myself to sleep.

eleven

The day is sweltering. The air is so heavy with moisture, my lungs grow tired just breathing. It's too hot to be in my truck, or directly under the sun, so I find a tree and sit under it, staying in the shade as the ball of fire overhead crawls across the sky.

Around noon, I pull out two slices of bread, spreading some of the peanut butter on them. When I try to retrieve the thick PB from the jar, the plastic knife from the grocery store breaks in two. Now I have to use my fingers to spread the peanut butter around. It's such a small thing, but it makes me want to cry.

As if the world has turned on me. As if it's a slight from the universe. As if the cosmos is treating me like the punch line of a bad joke.

Like the cosmos cares one way or the other.

But it doesn't.

I eat. Then I lie back against the tree, watching people mill about. Living their lives. Carefree. I used to move day-to-day without a care. I had no idea how good I had it.

The heat is overwhelming, and I start to nod off.

Some part of my consciousness whispers that it's not too late to go back to Russell. To beg him to take me back. To let him use me, and I'll use him. Like two parasites, going at each other back and forth. Or two snakes devouring one another.

Slowly, I sit up and shake off the thought. I have too much pride to go back. To him, or to my dad, or to Texas. I want to fix things on my own. Or is that my pride lying to me? Maybe it's my pride that got me here, and I need to let it go to get out of this situation.

After the sun takes its final bow for the day, dipping below the city horizon, I make my way back to my truck. When I get there, I don't turn it on. I can't afford to use the AC. Not when the gas is almost gone. Instead, I crawl over the tailgate, sit in the bed, and pull out my wallet. I count out the dollar bills left. One five-dollar bill and six one-dollar bills. Eleven dollars. It won't go far. Right now, I have eleven dollars. I'm richer today than I will be tomorrow.

I don't want to think about it.

But I have to think about it.

How do I survive on eleven dollars?

coins

Two nights I've slept in my truck.

Three days I've wandered the streets.

Tonight I'll run out of bread and peanut butter. I already ran out of water. I have two bananas left.

I don't want to spend my last eleven dollars. But I don't see a way around it. And after? What then?

My gut churns. I'm not sure if it's from hunger, or anxiety, or both.

I walk down the sidewalk, staring into restaurant windows. I try not to fixate on the plates of food, even as my mouth waters.

Waiting to cross the street at a red light, I notice a single penny on the sidewalk. If a coin is heads up, it's supposed to be good luck. This coin happens to be tails, butt-side up. I pick it up anyway. There's no such thing as lucky for me anymore.

Moving along, I scan the ground for more coins. Pennies, nickels, dimes, anything.

Walking past a pay phone, I think back to being a kid,

always sticking my finger in the change return slot in case I found nickels or dimes that would buy me gum or allow me to play an arcade game. I stick my finger in the opening, but there's nothing.

Then I notice a laundromat. Trying not to draw any attention to myself, I stride in as if I belong there. Slyly, I meander from machine to machine, searching out left-behind quarters. I finally discover one hiding just beneath a machine.

Outside, I squeeze the coin, pressing George Washington's face into my palm, when I notice a street vendor on the corner. He's selling fresh fruit. BANANAS 25¢ reads a handmade sign. A single quarter can buy me a banana?

A banana is a whole meal to me now.

I trade the coin for the yellow fruit and slip it into my backpack for later. In my backpack is my empty water bottle. I'm thirsty. I've been thirsty all day, sweating out my moisture under the diabolical sun.

But I keep walking. I am getting desperate when I hear the laughter of children. At a playground nearby, small boys and girls swing on swing sets and slide down slides. And within the park is a water fountain. I drink and I drink and I drink until my stomach grows tight with fullness. I fill up my bottle and stow it in my backpack with the rest of my food.

I memorize where the park is, so I can come back.

At least one thing is free.

snacks

Bourbon Street is packed with people drinking, laughing, roaring, dancing on the cobblestones. Inside, the bars are packed with tourists and locals alike, ordering cheap drinks. It's happy hour.

I don't know why I return here to the crowds, except that it's somehow comforting to be around people. I spent all day hiding in the shade, in my head, trying to figure out what to do. But my thoughts go in circles. Thinking is starting to seem hard.

Everything is starting to seem too hard.

Too impossible.

I'm leaning against a column, watching a gay bar across the street. Through the windows, I see friends hugging hello, ordering drinks, cheering. I imagine the clinking of glasses, and being inside, being one of them.

A bartender refills a basket of pretzels. The clientele munches on them absent-mindedly. As if they're nothing. When the basket goes empty, the bartender refills it again.

And it occurs to me.

When the door guy finally gets up and disappears inside to use the restroom, I walk in hurriedly, so I won't be caught and carded. I take the last seat at the bar, where I order a water. When the bartender raises an eyebrow, I say, "I'm waiting for my boyfriend."

The bartender drops off a glass of ice water. Just touching the glass, my fingers note that I haven't felt this kind of cold in days. I never before realized what a luxury ice was. I have to stop myself from gulping it down.

I remind myself to be casual. To act like everybody else. To pick at the free pretzels slowly. My hunger doesn't want to allow that kind of self-control, forcing a struggle with my own animal instincts. I study the signature knot of the symmetrical loop in one pretzel, and wonder who came up with that, and how they make pretzels so tiny. Then I nibble at it, dissecting it with my teeth. Like a beaver at a log. Chipping away at it, trying to make it last. Rolling the texture over in my mouth, admiring the salt on my tongue.

The bartender gives me a few sharp looks. He doesn't say anything, but anytime he walks past me, I feel like a thief. I'm taking up a seat at his bar, meaning one less customer for him, one less tip.

After half an hour, the bartender comes back around. "You gonna order anything?"

"Sorry. Still waiting for my boyfriend."

He doesn't believe me. But he doesn't realize my game either, cause he refills the pretzels and returns to another customer waving him down from the front of the bar. When he isn't looking, I take a handful of pretzels and shove them into my pocket. Then a second.

This will be my dinner later.

For now, I sit here casually, finishing the pretzels. Until every salty crumb is gone.

I feel like I've hit the jackpot. And I feel stupid I hadn't thought of this sooner.

―――――

Walking down Bourbon Street the next day, my stomach trembling from not having eaten since last night, I return to the same bar. Inside, the same bartender is making drinks. I realize I can't pull the same trick twice, not two days in a row.

So I saunter down the street, scanning doors for doormen. When I see a restaurant without one, I head inside and go to the bar. No snacks. I walk out.

When I see another empty doorway to a bar, I step inside. I'm scared of getting caught. And it must show, cause a manager stops me. "Can I see your ID?"

Hoping he'll let it slide, I pull out my wallet, handing him my driver's license. He scans it. "You're underage. I need to ask you to leave."

At the next bar, it happens again. I'm caught, IDed, and pointed toward the exit.

I wonder what I'm doing wrong.

I study the street and its crowds, watching people move in and out of bars with abandon. Most of them are drunk, but there's a certainty in their steps. They have a purpose. They have confidence. They look like they belong. It helps if they're in a crowd.

Scanning the bar entrances, I wait for a group of tourists. A cluster of loud women appear. They're all dolled up, wearing tight dresses. Except the one in the white veil, the one with a necklace of plastic penises and a tiara that says BRIDE.

"Let's go in here!" one of them shouts gleefully, leading the pack. I move in close behind, and meld with the back end of the bachelorette party. I add my laughter to one of their jokes, and follow them in. The doorman doesn't even notice me.

When they go straight to the crowded bar, I go with them. When they order drinks, I order a water. The bartender doesn't think twice. While she pours frozen margaritas for the others, I dig into the bucket of popcorn on the counter. I'm three handfuls in by the time she returns with my water. When the women cheer the soon-to-be bride, I cheer with them.

———

Happy hour arrives again. I patrol the streets, looking in windows, scanning bar counters for my next free meal.

For some reason, the straight bars are harder for me to get into. But the gay bar doormen are more lax. Especially if I walk in with confidence. And with a group. I do this by simply walking a few inches closer than I should. It feels intimate. And I smile, trying to match the mood of my queer peers.

I target three friends. They're all dressed like one another. Khaki shorts and pastel polos. Collars popped up. I'm thankful I'm wearing my polo shirt, and I pop up the collar too. Then I sidle up behind the men, and laugh when they laugh. The doorman doesn't even look in my direction.

Even though it's early, a DJ is spinning, the bass thumping. Remixes of familiar pop songs play through the speakers. I recognize a Madonna song "Ray of Light." When some of the crew I came in after start moving to the music, I mimic them, swaying my shoulders. I follow them to the far end of the bar. When I see trail mix in a bowl, I try not to grab. Instead, I take a handful casually, and toss it back piece by piece. I savor every morsel. I remember reading somewhere that nuts have protein, and I almost laugh when I think this is the healthiest meal I've had in days.

One of the guys notices me. "You following me?"

"What? No."

"Relax. I was just kidding." He smiles from behind his glasses. "Whatcha drinking?"

"Just water," I say.

"Screw water. I'm offering to buy you a drink. What do you want?" He smiles. He's Russell's age, and for a second I cringe. But he's not Russell. And I won't make the same mistake twice.

So I say, "Ginger ale."

The guy rolls his eyes, and turns to the bartender. "Two vodka sodas."

When the drinks come, the guy pushes one into my hand. "I'm John."

"Rex."

"Great name," he says. "Is Rex short for anything?"

"Nope, just Rex."

"Well, nice to meet you, Just Rex."

He clinks my glass with his, and we both drink. I feel my face contort. It must have been a heavy pour, cause all I can taste is vodka. John laughs at me.

"Not a big drinker?"

"Not exactly."

"Well, drink slow, then." John takes a sip of his own, eyeing me over the rim. Then he leans in, his lips at my ear, so I can hear him over the music, and asks, "You're underage, aren't you?"

"Nope."

He grins. "Uh-huh. Okay."

We both laugh.

He leans in again, saying, "Your secret is safe with me."

"Who's this?" one of John's friend's asks.

"An old acquaintance," John says. He winks at me. "Cameron, this is Rex. Rex, Cameron. And that's Greg."

"Nice to meet you." We shake hands.

Then Cameron says, "Let's liven things up a little. Come on."

John takes my free hand and leads me back toward the men's room. I pause. "But I don't need to pee."

John smiles smugly. "Neither do we." He pulls me into the bathroom, into the far end stall with his two friends. With the four of us crammed in here, John standing over the toilet, and the toilet paper roll jammed into my leg, it's more than crowded. This close to three strangers, I feel vulnerable. I think of Russell, of me telling him to stop, and my stomach quakes. Why did these three men invite me in here?

I think I'm in trouble. I'm about to excuse myself when Cameron pulls out a little plastic baggie with white powder in it. With his other hand, he pulls out his car keys.

"What is that?" I ask.

"Just a little blow," Cameron says. He snorts a tiny hill of powder off the tip of his key. "Want some?"

"I'll stick with my vodka soda," I say.

"Party pooper," Cameron says, taking another snort. He passes the bag and the key to John.

John does a bump. He holds up the bag and the key for me. "You sure?"

"Yeah, I'm good. Thank you."

Cameron is sniffing and sniffing, trying to clear his nose. He rubs white powder from his nostril with his thumb, then licks it off.

But Cameron keeps sniffing. This time cause he smells something. He leans over to me and takes a whiff. "You stink."

————

I watch an old house from the cab of my truck. The lights aren't on. They haven't been on all night while I've been here. I don't think anyone is home. So when the lights go out at the house next door, I slip out of my truck.

Duffel bag in hand, I creep over.

I hop the fence, into the backyard.

I peer inside the windows. Still dark. No sounds. No dog. Not even a cat. Not that I can see from outside.

Walking as quiet as I'm able, I find what I'm looking for: a water hose.

Taking my clothes out of the duffel bag, I soak them, scrub the smelly parts together, rinse them, then twist out the water. I wash everything I've worn, underwear, socks, shirts.

Usually I would be terrified to expose myself in public. But I haven't showered in a week. And I feel disgusting. I need this. I look around, as if asking for permission. There's no one here but grasshoppers singing.

I strip naked.

Then I turn the hose on myself, trying to wash away the

scent of the last week. Scrubbing under my armpits, soaking my hair, scouring my face, wiping at my chest, shoulders, and back. The hot night air fades in the presence of the cool splashing against my skin. My feet squish into dirt-made-mud, blades of grass springing up between my toes.

Under the moon, I hold the hose over my head, letting the water drench my body, rinse over every inch of me, until I feel clean.

truck

In New Orleans, a multimillion-dollar residence can be located next to a dilapidated house that's falling apart at the seams. Neighborhoods are like a checkerboard of new and old, beautiful and destitute. So when I find an abandoned house in a decent area, I park in its driveway.

I lock my stuff in the cab, then climb into the bed of my truck. It's not as secure for me in the back, but it's certainly less hot than inside. Sometimes there's even a breeze. I also have room to spread out, though the metal ridges of the floor make it uncomfortable. Still, when it's not overcast I can see the sky.

Two nights in a row, I camp here. During the day, I leave my truck to wander around, looking for work, water, and shade. I only have a few gallons of gas left in the tank, so I move it only when I have to. But I can't park here forever. I know that. Sooner or later, someone will notice. Someone will have it towed. Then what would I do without it?

This truck is the only home I have right now. It's not much, but it's mine.

I'm so hungry, though. I can't help considering the option to sell it. I might even get a few thousand for it. I'd be able to feed myself for a while, maybe get a motel room to live in. But then what? Try to get a job again? There's no guarantee I'd be hired. Try to get a place? With no job, I wouldn't be able to afford rent after a few months.

The scales balance in my head, rocking up and down on either side, considering which weighs heavier, which move is smarter. Keep the truck, or sell the truck? A full meal sounds so good right now. But if I sell it, and I can't get a job, then I'm only stalling the inevitable. And I wouldn't have the truck anymore.

My stomach says yes. But logic says no. It'd be a bad idea. Right now the truck is a connection to my old life. A security blanket. An escape if I need it . . .

And I do need it. To escape.

Except I don't have money for gas. And even if I did, I don't know where I'd go.

I'm stuck here.

I try to think of someplace I could drive to on the gas I have left. But my thoughts are all twisted up by the hunger I feel all over my body. I want to cry, but I can't even afford to lose tears. I can't afford to give up any moisture. Not in this heat.

Still, I can't afford to keep driving my truck around. Eventually it'd run out of gas. No, I have to park it somewhere safe. Where my truck won't be towed. Where it will be waiting for me when I need it.

Suddenly I recall my job orientation at the Walmart in Prattville. That we were told the front of the parking lot was reserved for customers. That all employees should park in the back of the lot.

The next evening, I drive to the nearest Walmart open twenty-four hours. I steer the truck to the back of the lot and park. I sit there for a while, watching people in blue vests get out of their cars and walk toward the superstore entrance.

When no one is around, I get out of my truck. I take out my duffel bag and backpack, then lock the doors. Looking at my truck, I want to cry, like I'm leaving a friend behind. Like I'm leaving it alone, in a foreign place, with no way to protect itself.

Even as I grow sick to my stomach, I force myself to walk away. To return to downtown New Orleans, where the bars are, where the tourists are, where I feel less alone.

I wish I'd stayed in Alabama. I wish I'd stayed at my job, where I could count on a paycheck. I wish I'd slept in my truck in the Walmart parking lot there until I found a way to get an apartment. But wishes aren't real. They're just thoughts fighting against you. Fighting against reality.

Wishes aren't going to get me anything.

shelter

The glow of streetlights interrupts the darkness. Under the illumination, several bugs dance about, as if rejoicing.

A man wanders by, his wild hair white, wearing a camo green army jacket. His dirty pants are several sizes too big. He has to reach behind to hike them up every few steps before they fall again cause he doesn't have a belt. He's not wearing any shoes.

I recognize him. I've seen him before. Begging for change. Digging in trash cans for food. But right now he's moving with a purpose, driven by something strong. He's talking to himself, muttering something about food. I follow him.

He turns one block and then the next. Then he joins a procession of other homeless men and women making their way into a building. It's a church.

I consider how churches receive my kind. How they feel about gay people. How they hate me just for being born.

I almost walk away.

Until I catch the scent of food. My stomach quivers. So I get in line.

Inside, three rows of tables line the center of the room. At the far end, two women hand out small trays of food. Meat loaf, green beans, a slice of white bread. There's fruit punch in large orange coolers. I crane my neck to look down the line of people, observing tattered clothes and dirty faces. Pride rears up inside me. Like I'm too good for this. But I don't have any choice in the matter. Hunger overrules my arrogance.

It takes all my willpower not to shove the food into my mouth as soon as the woman hands me my tray. But I manage to wait until I sit down.

Everyone eats fast. Some with their fingers. Some with the plastic forks provided. The smell of the man sitting next to me is too much. He reeks of urine and body odor. I pick up my tray and move to the next row, where another stench greets me. At this point, I'm too hungry to care. I eat.

The meat loaf is the best I've ever had. The same with the green beans. With the bread I sop up the juices left behind. I realize I haven't washed my hands. But I don't care. I find myself licking the plate, making sure every bit is inside me.

"Would you like seconds?" a man in preacher's clothing asks.

Reluctantly, I nod.

He directs me back toward the line. Everyone is getting seconds. The next round of food overfills my stomach, making it ache. I feel like I might burst. This is the first full meal I've had since I left Russell's. It's been maybe a week? I don't know. My days have started to bleed into one another.

The preacher is making the rounds, talking to the homeless one person at a time. I hear words like "Jesus Christ" and "salvation" and "heaven," and aggravation rolls through me. I duck my head low and walk toward the door.

One of female volunteers stops me. Gently, she asks, "Do you have someplace to sleep tonight?"

Slowly, I shake my head.

"We have cots in the next room. A clean bathroom you can use. And breakfast in the morning."

I nod toward the preacher. "Do I have to get saved?"

She shakes her head no. "We would love for you to join our congregation, but it's not necessary. We just want to give you a place to rest your head."

My pride takes another hit as I say, "Okay."

———

I toss and turn.

The room is cold. Even under the blanket they gave me, I'm freezing. The snoring doesn't help. On the other side of the room, a man snores like a freight train, his breathing heavy and labored. Someone else is sniffling every few seconds. The room isn't big enough to hold this many cots, this many people, so I hear every sound.

Finally, I start to drift off.

The sound of movement stirs my mind from a soft dream. I wake with a start to find a man taking my shoes out from under my cot. I kick him in the head. "Get the fuck away from my stuff."

"Shhhhh," someone hisses.

As my eyes adjust to the dark, I see the thief. He's old, frail. He looks startled by my kick, maybe confused by his own actions. He totters to the other end of the dark room, crawls into a corner, and rocks back and forth.

I put my shoes on, and tie the laces tight. I double-knot them. I bind my backpack and duffel bag together with their straps, put them at my feet, and stick a leg through the handle. If someone's going to try to take my stuff, I won't make it easy.

I don't get good sleep. I keep waiting for someone to rob me. Or attack me. I was getting better sleep outside. And every time I wake up, the old man is still rocking back and forth. Back and forth. Moaning. Like a ghost of who he used to be.

cardboard

There are plenty of places to sleep. But I like public parks.

In Alabama, insects sang outside my open screened window. Here, natural sounds are replaced by the city's music of police sirens and drunk tourists and jazz music in the not-so-far distance. There's sometimes a cool breeze in the open air. There are other people around, so I don't feel quite by myself. And the benches are surprisingly comfortable. Though tonight they're all occupied, so I find a spot on the grass near a set of shrubs.

It's a clear night, and a few stars manage to outshine the reflection of the city's glow. The constellation Orion is among them. He's my favorite. He followed me from Texas to Alabama, and now to New Orleans.

I lie on my back, staring up at the stars that make up Orion's belt, and remember camping when I was a little boy. My parents had already divorced, but they still lived in the same town. On weekends, my dad would come pick me up, take me to the woods with his college friends. They would drink beer, while I lay on the ground, looking up at the sky, pretending I was watching the heroes of Greek myth.

Strong Hercules wrestled the Nemean lion, and sly Odysseus blinded the cyclops. Parent gods Zeus and Hera fought for the love of humans, yet punished those who did not bow at their altars. Half-man, half-goat, Pan sang his songs from a flute, delighting those around him, even Artemis, goddess of the hunt. But my favorite was brave Perseus, who gathered the weapons necessary to defeat snake-haired Medusa.

Though I always felt sorry for Medusa. She had no say in her curse to change all living things to stone with but a glance. Her existence must have been a solitary one, left alone in her temple. Until her head was chopped clean off from her neck.

"Get up," a gruff voice sounds. "You can't sleep here."

Two policemen are strutting around, prodding those sleeping with their nightsticks. Then the officer points at me. "Come on. Up and at 'em."

I pretend to be sleep. Maybe if I don't say anything—

A foot hits my side. It's less than a kick, but more than a nudge. "Hey. You listening? Out of here."

"I'm just sleeping," I say. "Where's the harm in that?"

"You giving me lip?" the first officer asks. He pokes me hard with his nightstick. "Up. Get moving. Now."

I push myself off the ground. I put on my backpack, sling my duffel over my shoulder. I mutter, "Asshole."

The cop grabs my collar. "What'd you say?"

There's rage in his eyes. The same rage I've seen in my father's eyes. In my stepfather's eyes. It's a look that only men know how to give. One that says they're willing to hurt another person to prove they're better. That they're an alpha.

Sick of feeling powerless, I stand my ground, saying, "I called you an asshole."

The cop raises his nightstick.

I brace myself for impact when the second officer grabs his arm. "Dude, chill out. He's just a kid."

The first cop studies my face for a moment. He lets go of my collar, then immediately shoves me away. "Get outta here. Stupid punk."

I wander after the others. We move like the walking dead. Zombies. Shuffling along, every one of us hungry and tired. Not just from being woken, but tired of every day repeating itself. The search for clean water, for food, for a bathroom, for a place to sleep. When we find those places, we make a mental note, and go back until someone tells us we can't.

Two blocks away, I'm still looking for somewhere to rest. One woman goes behind a dumpster, fishing out massive rectangles of broken-down cardboard boxes. She drags them to the other end of the alley, stacks them one on top of the other. Then lies down on top of them.

I ask, "Is that comfortable?"

"Better than the asphalt," she says.

"You mind if I—"

"Knock yourself out," she says. Rolling over, she curls into a ball. Like a child. Reminding me that she was once a baby, needing her diaper changed, sucking on her thumb, waiting for a bottle or breast to provide her milk. Just like everyone else. But that was before she grew up. Before the world cast her out. Before she was lost.

Lost like me.

From behind the dumpster, I pull out several layers of cardboard. I make my way farther down the alley, off the beaten path, away from where the cops might see me. I pile the brown flattened boxes on top of one another. Then I lie down. It's not as comfortable as the grass and the soft dirt of the parks. But it is better than the asphalt. I try to be grateful for that.

nightmares

I sleep. But I don't get good sleep.

Not in parks, not on benches, not in alleys. Not when I'm alone. Not when I have to sleep with one eye open. Not when I'm worried about cops, or being attacked, or someone robbing me.

I don't know who would want to steal my backpack or my duffel bag or my empty wallet, but someone might . . . So I don't sleep.

Not really. Instead, I'm in and out of consciousness. Thoughts and memories morph into one another, then fade into colorful otherworlds or hellish landscapes with vicious demons that eventually transform into brick buildings or dumpsters or sidewalks near where I set up for the night. Every night, my dark dreams melt into thoughts about death and dying, and I wonder if I'll make it through until morning.

I worry about the dull ache in my muscles. About the tightness in my stomach. About the fogginess in my brain. About the pangs in my chest. Will I get sick? Will I starve to death? Or will my heart just give out?

Most nights, the darkness becomes tangible, presses down on me so I can't breathe. Then my dread and despair spiral in on themselves, over and over, coiling down into an abyss, infecting my thinking with serpents to convince me: This is it. I won't make it. I won't wake up tomorrow.

But then I do.

The sun always rises.

But one of these days, it will rise without me.

And I wonder, will it be soon?

Or will I grow old like this?

sign

I don't want to think of myself as one of them, but I can't deny that I am. We don't necessarily speak, instead we move past each other like lost ships. I see the same people again and again, with vacant eyes and grit dug into the lines on their faces. They often wear the same clothes, carry the same bags, push the same carts.

I've never wanted to beg. I don't believe in getting something for nothing. But my wallet is empty. I'm hungry. And my trick sneaking into bars doesn't work anymore. They know my face. People can smell it on me, the desperation, the stink of being unshowered. No matter how hard I've tried to keep my clothes clean, they're starting to show signs of wear.

Sitting on the side of the street, I'm finally caving—I'm making a sign.

Behind a restaurant, I find a box of cardboard decorated with smiling bananas. I break it apart, tearing off a rectangle. I have an old marker in my backpack. But I don't know what to write.

I think of the other signs I've seen:

HOMELESS AND HUNGRY

PLEASE HELP. GOD BLESS

SEEKING HUMAN KINDNESS

HOMELESS, NEED HELP

DESPERATE

TAKING DONATIONS

SUPERMODEL, OUT OF WORK

I HAVE A WIFE AND TWO KIDS. PLEASE, WE NEED YOUR HELP

CAN YOU PLEASE SPARE SOME CHANGE FOR ME? THANK YOU

VIETNAM VETERAN. NEED AID

WHY LIE, I WANT A BEER

WILL EAT FOR FOOD

I BET YOU $1 YOU WILL READ THIS SIGN

LOST JOB + APARTMENT. ALONE. NO FAMILY. GRATEFUL FOR ANY
THING

WILL WORK FOR FOOD

PLEASE GIVE ME A JOB

NO JOB. THREE KIDS & A DOG. PLEASE HELP

VERY EMBARRASSED, BUT MUST ASK FOR HELP. DON'T KNOW
WHAT ELSE TO DO

DOWN AT THE BOTTOM. HELP PLEASE

CLEAN + SOBER. FEED ME

TOO UGLY TO PROSTITUTE! TRAVELING AND NEED FUNDS

ONCE I WAS LIKE YOU

There're too many variations to count. I sway back and forth between writing something clever or something serious. I wonder which will get me more money, and I have no idea. The longer I wait, the more shame builds up in me like poison, stinging my weak muscles. I don't want to ask for help. I don't want to beg. But I have to.

Eventually, I write: JOB. FOOD. WATER. ANYTHING HELPS. THANK YOU.

I tuck the sign underneath my arm and start walking to find a spot. I discover an intersection with a ton of foot traffic. But there's already someone sitting there with a sign. It reads: LET'S DO BRUNCH. U BUY.

His hair is wild, sticking out in all directions. A bushy beard hides the lower half of his face, so I can't tell if he's thirty or sixty, though his eyes seem older. He wears a blanket around his neck, as if he were expecting cold weather. I think he's wearing black shoes, until I realize he has no shoes on. Not even socks. His feet are pure black.

I don't know what the proper etiquette is. I know I can't sit beside him. So I cross the street and take the opposite corner. I sit down. I take off my hat and put it between my feet, turned up like a catcher's mitt hoping to catch money.

As people walk by, I watch them. But I can't do it for long. I don't want to meet their gaze. I don't want them to see me.

So I look down.

The sidewalk is filthy. One spot is sticky with beer. A piece of gum has become a flattened black coin-sized pancake sealed onto the concrete. An ant makes its journey beneath me. Searching for food, like me. But it has a home to go to. A home full of other ants. A family.

After only a few minutes, my shirt is soaked with sweat. I'm baking under the sun. Across the street, the other guy is in the shade. He's clearly smarter than me, or at least has more common sense. Even with his plaid shirt turned brown, holes in his pants, fingernails black with soot, he knows to stay out of the sun. Then I feel sorry, having judged him by how he looks. Cause now I wonder how I must look to the people passing by.

―――――

My hat is still empty.

I glance up every once in a while, wondering if people don't see me or don't care. I realize, the thing about sitting on the side of the street with a sign asking for help? I become invisible to almost everyone. People try not to look at me. They move their eyes away in another direction.

I want to be furious. But I can't judge them.

I used to do the same thing.

fireworks

I know it's July. And that today is Friday. Or maybe Saturday? I know cause there's always more tourists on weekend nights than weekday nights. But I'm not sure of the actual date—not until the sky explodes in bursts of light and sound.

The booming erupts into fantastic colors, into exotic flowers that spray outward until dissolving as they rain down, vanishing before they touch the earth.

I feel like a kid again, marveling at the magic.

Lowering my eyes from the sky to the crowds, I notice all the people gazing up in wonder. At the darkness interrupted by red and blue and white and green and yellow and orange and purple. The lights splash across their faces, creating a kaleidoscope of brilliant sparkles that reflects in the eyes of tourists and locals and homeless alike.

During the light show, I forget myself. Lost in the moment, watching the sky with the rest of the people, I'm just another person on this planet.

One of so many.

I'm part of something bigger . . .

The fireworks become fast and furious. Flashes and sparkles paint the sky, while booming so loud I can feel them in my ears. And just as I think the heavens will burst into flame . . . it' s over.

Night takes back the atmosphere, and there's no trace of the celebration except for plumes of smoke rising up and dissipating.

Then the audience falls to pieces, disintegrating into couples and families and groups of friends. Some will go to restaurants, others to bars, the rest will return to their homes or hotels where they will sleep in beds.

Me? I'm going to stay here for a while. I have no place to go.

happy meal

Despite sitting in the shadow of a building, I am still cooking in the heat. Tying and untying my shoelaces over and over again, just so I have something to do, I can't tell exactly how long I've been sitting here today. The only way I really know that time is passing is the movement of the sun across the sky. That, and the way the tourists go from sober to tipsy to drunk.

I've grown to love the sound, *clink*. It means one coin is landing and hitting another coin. I glance up to see a small pile of silver and copper growing in my hat. I don't count it yet, not wanting to be disappointed with the income.

Clink-clink-clink. I like the rapid-succession sound even more. It means someone just emptied their pocket or purse into my hat. Quarters and dimes and nickels and pennies. I look up to the generous giver and say, "Thanks. I really appreciate it."

There's no sound when someone drops paper cash into my hat. I keep an eye out, though, making sure to thank the person. When a dollar bill floats down, I quickly snatch it from the hat to hide it in my pocket as if the wind might steal away my prize.

After another hour, I still haven't counted. But already I suspect I'll have enough for food tonight. My stomach rumbles at the thought.

But is that what I'll spend the money on? I need to be practical, think through my options first. I could use the money to put gas in my truck's tank, but I still have nowhere to go. My body is home to an acrid stench that is starting to burn my own nose. Maybe I should buy deodorant. But what good would that do? In a few days I'd stink again anyway. Or I could use my quarters to go to a laundromat and wash my clothes, which are also starting to reek on account of the hot, humid days.

I recall the smell of detergent and fabric softener, of me as a little boy accompanying my mom to the laundry room of our apartment complex. She would bring a bag of quarters, those that she had saved up, to feed the washers and dryers. I always wanted to steal that bag of coins, and go to the arcade to play video games. I didn't understand how precious twenty-five cents really was. How valuable every dollar was. Or how lucky I truly was when my mom took me to McDonald's and bought me a Happy Meal.

As a kid, nothing made me happier. The small paper box with the golden arches as handles. The outside showed games and cartoons. Ronald McDonald and Grimace and the Fry Guys and the Hamburglar. The box's roof would unfold to reveal the contents: a burger, fries, and a prize, usually a toy, to take home and play with for hours.

I smile at the memory. Then, deep inside, a nostalgic desire rises up in my stomach. I want to go to McDonald's.

Buying myself a Happy Meal wouldn't be right. Not when I can buy a lot more food for the same price. Food that would last for more than one meal. A loaf of bread. Peanut butter. Bananas. But the fantasy overtakes me. I think, What about happiness? Isn't a few minutes of total joy worth it? I've had so many bananas that I hate them now. The taste. The texture. The temperature. But bananas are cheap and easy.

They're not like a McDonald's Happy Meal. The crisp, salted fries. The juicy burger, with the slice of cheese, between the soft buns. Even with this humidity, I want the hot food in my mouth. It means its fresh, just off the grill, right out of the fryer, and straight into my maw. And the prize. The toy.

I have no idea what it would be. But the idea of something new? Something to call my own? Some colorful trinket wrapped in plastic, a present for me to open?

Fuck the cost.

I know what I'm buying if I have enough.

————

In the McDonald's bathroom, I wash my hands four times. I want to make sure they're clean before I eat.

Waiting in line in front of me, a boy stands with his mother. He keeps craning his neck around to glance at me, like he's caught me cause I shouldn't be here. He wears a striped shirt, red and white, red and white, red and white. The shirt is so clean, the white gleams. So different from the clothes I'm wearing.

I try to shove down my envy over another thing that I used to take for granted: clean clothes.

I feel eyes on me from the other customers. Whether they're

real or imagined, it doesn't matter. I'm self-conscious. I try to will the customers to make their purchases faster.

When I get to the front of the line, I'm as polite as I can be when I order. "One Happy Meal, please."

The cashier surveys me, on the verge of saying that I'm not a kid. Instead, she smiles gently and asks, "Chicken nuggets or a cheeseburger?"

"Cheeseburger, please."

"What do you want to drink with that?"

I forgot a drink came with it. "A Coke."

I count out my dollar bills, quarters, dimes, and pennies, until I have the right amount. I hand it to her, not even the slightest bit reluctant. A moment later, she returns with the box of delight. It's every bit as colorful as I'd hoped.

I take it and find a corner booth away from everyone else. I can't wipe the grin off my face. Disney's *Mulan* is on the exterior of the box. I remember seeing the trailer for it the last time I went to the movies. That was before the beach, before the talk with my dad, before—

I shake my head, trying to push away the yesterdays.

Instead, I stare down the golden arches that top the box. Slowly, I pull them apart, invoking memories of Happy Meals from the past. The aroma of food drifts up, into my nose. Already I'm salivating like a dog.

Like a Christmas present, I unwrap the waxy paper to reveal a burger. I bite into it, savoring the mouthfeel. Then I follow with a french fry. And then another. The taste hasn't changed at all. I sip Coke through my straw, then return to the fries, and then the burger. I try to take it slow, to appreciate every bite. But it's gone too fast.

Still, I left the best for last . . .

I fish in the box and withdraw a small plastic bag. I pry it open with my fingers, and retrieve a small red dragon. According to the box, its name is Mushu. For a long while, I stare, turning him over in my hands, as if I were a child again, innocent and easily delighted.

Dragons are lucky, aren't they? The phrase "luck dragon" comes to mind. Pushing through the fog of memory, I recall a white-furred beast with the face of a dog that could fly. It was Falkor, a luck dragon, from *The Neverending Story*. When I was seven or eight, I'd watch the movie over and over on a VHS tape, wishing I could have just such a magical creature . . .

Now I do.

I decide then and there that I need all the luck I can get. And Mushu? If I treat him right, Mushu will bring me some.

bathroom

1

When I wake up, the first thing I do is pull Mushu from my pocket.

"Good morning," I whisper to the plastic figure. I stroke him, give him a kiss on the forehead, then place him back in my pocket.

I sit up on my cardboard mat and untie my duffel bag and backpack from my leg. I yawn, then stand up and stretch. The day is overcast, and I'm hoping that means it'll be cooler. But the cloud cover will probably just make it more humid.

My stomach growls.

I've always heard breakfast is the most important meal of the day. It gets the next twenty-four hours started right. Your stomach is full, so you can think and focus on what needs to get done. Even if all that needs to get done is the search for your next meal.

But most mornings, for me, there's no breakfast in sight.

The shelter kitchen is closed mornings unless you spend

the night. And at night they only have so many beds. So no cot means no free breakfast. And no breakfast means I'm going to wander around with an aching stomach.

To distract myself, I follow my new routine.

I make my way to the park, to the public restroom. There are three stalls and three sinks. The smell is horrific cause the first toilet is clogged with feces and toilet paper. That doesn't keep others from using it. In the third stall, I take my time, trying to shit in peace, but someone bangs at the door. Still, it doesn't take much time. Not much comes out on account of the singular meager meal I had the day before. But at least there's toilet paper. I try to be grateful for that much.

I walk over to the sink. Reluctantly, I set my backpack and duffel bag on the wet, nasty tiled floor.

In the mirror, I see soot on my face, and wonder how it got there. Sleeping on cardboard, maybe, the dark ink from the recycled box rubbing off on my cheek in the night. Or perhaps it's from touching something dirty, then wiping the sweat from my brow. I wonder how long the grime has been there. Embarrassment rinses over me.

I want to stay clean. I really do. To stay looking like I don't belong on the street. But isn't that just denial at this point? I don't have access to an unsullied bathroom. Or a washing machine and dryer. Without washing them, despite trying to be careful, my shorts and shirts are filthy. Probably from sitting and sleeping on the streets of New Orleans.

I go to wash my hands. There's no soap. The soap is always out.

I take off my shirt. I splash water on my face, scrubbing with my fingers until I appear clean. Then, under my arms, I wipe myself down with a paper towel. I can't reach my back, so I'm left to wonder how disgusting it's become.

I desperately wish I could have a bath. Or a shower. Or just a body of water to dunk myself into.

I think of summer days spent in pools as a kid. Whether it was a public pool, an apartment pool, or a pool behind a friend's house. There was always access to beat the Texas heat. I'd rip off my shirt and sandals, then run barefoot across steaming concrete toward the deep end, where I would climb a ladder to cannonball off the diving board. I'd challenge other swimmers to race, sometimes underwater to see if I could hold my breath for the length of the pool. I'd splash and spit water at friends, or play Marco Polo, or Fish Out of Water. I'd refuse to get out of the pool when my mom called me. I was addicted to the refreshing nature of the clear, cool water.

But there's no pool here. Just a grimy bathroom with broken tiles and exposed rusted pipes, and a line of people waiting to piss and miss the toilet.

These waist-up hand baths help, but in this bathroom I don't dare take off my shoes. That means I can't take off my shorts. So I can't wash myself, not entirely. I refuse to get naked here in a public restroom. Not like the guy two sinks down from me. Pants and underwear around his ankles, he shamelessly scrubs at his groin, genitals flopping around.

I tell myself, I'm not there yet. I'm not there.

Not yet.

fries

No one is donating to my hat.

Some days, no one gives up any money. Some days, my sign goes unnoticed or just plain ignored. Sometimes I'm sitting in the wrong spot. Other times it's cause there's too little foot traffic. Today there're too many others on the street begging for change. There are not enough coins or dollars to go around.

My stomach aches. Like my intestines are knotted in on themselves. Like they're being choked by two strong hands plunged into my body to torture me. My gut makes weird noises, as if calling out. I think back to when I was young, reading my mom's *Time* magazines, pictures of all those kids in Africa covered in flies, bellies extended from lack of food. They weren't hungry. They were starving.

I tell myself, I'm not starving. Somehow, I manage.

It's just so weird, such a mindfuck, being surrounded by restaurants and grocery stores, and having no way to access regular meals. Like being locked in a cage with the keys just out of reach.

I rub Mushu for luck. Rubbing it again and again. Trying to garner some luck from its plastic body. But after what feels like hours, I give up. Thirty-seven cents is all I have to show for my patience.

I find a woman selling fruit at the corner of a street intersection and buy a banana. I hate these yellow fruits now. I'm so sick of eating them. But they're food. I peel the banana, careful not to touch it with my dirty fingers. I devour it. It isn't much of a lunch, but it's something.

Then I wander. Up one side of the street, down another, searching for a new spot to hold up my sign. My feet hurt, my shoes worn down. The day goes by with the sun breathing down on me, starting to burn my cheeks and ears. My back is all sweat beneath my baggage. And my armpits stink of body odor. I try to recall what my last real shower felt like, and I can't.

Day turns into night, and without breakfast, without a real lunch, my stomach is trembling again. It's always hungry, like a baby that keeps crying. My sole purpose each day is trying to feed it. To satiate the rolling pain. But I can't.

I think, This is my life now. I'm stuck. I'm never getting off the street. I'll never find a job. Never have money again. Never have the security of a home. Of a family. Of a shelter. I'll never know love again. Or the touch of someone who cares. This is all there is.

I feel like crying. Like screaming. Like lying down in the middle of the street and never getting up again.

Instead, I rub the lucky dragon in my pocket. I pull it out, squeeze it in my palm. Drift my thumb over the ridges of its spine. Examine the red color of its skin. I try to imagine sitting on a couch, watching TV with Mushu on the screen. I've never seen the movie it's in. But I want to pretend one day I will. That it's not impossible. That one day I'll be off the street.

Until then, I have to feed myself.

I remember the Happy Meal that Mushu came in. McDonald's is at a busy intersection, so I make my way there. The comforting glow of the golden arches beckons me. I take my seat outside, leaning against the building, hold up my sign, and turn my hat upside down, as if it's an extension of my hands, pleading. And I pray to my dragon that I'll make enough change to buy another Happy Meal. That I can get a friend for Mushu.

But after hours of waiting, I only have a dollar and sixty-four cents. And the crowds are diminishing. McDonald's will be closed soon.

Three teenage girls come out of the fast-food restaurant. Each girl has a paper bag, and is dipping her hand in and out, retrieving fries to eat.

"I have to stop eating these," the first girl says. "They're going to make me fat."

"But they're so good," the second says.

"Maybe you shouldn't have gotten the super-size, then," notes the third. "But don't waste the food. Eat it."

"No. No! I won't be tempted!" The first girl crumples up her bag and tosses it in the trash. The other two girls shrug, continuing their binge. Then the trio disappears into the shrinking crowd.

My eyes trail back to the trash can.

Should I?

It's free food.

I wander over to the trash and pick out her paper bag. I unfurl the top, and inside is a red carton of half-eaten fries. And they're still hot. One at a time, I shove them in my mouth, eating them all too quickly.

dinner

I saunter along St. Charles Avenue, admiring the beautiful live oaks and well-kept antebellum mansions. If the people who live in them have problems, it's more than likely they aren't worried about where their next meal will come from.

A *ding ding ding* sounds from the St. Charles streetcar as it crawls up its path toward me. The dark green trolley with crimson doors reminds me of . . . something. I can't remember. Lately, that's been happening a lot. Like my brain is only running at partial capacity.

I wish I could afford a ride, but I can't. So after the public transport passes, I step onto its track and raise my arms. I walk slowly, placing one foot in front of the other, each step on the metal rail, balancing as if on a tight rope, like I used to do when I was a kid, trying not to fall. My head feels light, almost drunk. A side effect of not eating today.

By the time I get to the French Quarter, the sky is beginning to dim. Wanting the comfort of music, I make my way to a gay bar and sit on the curb outside. My sign rests against my legs. I used to be one of those carefree people who walked in and out of places without any thought as to the privilege. It seems too ridiculous now, to not care more about all the little things.

Part of me worries that one of these days Russell will pass by on his way to a bar. Or maybe someone I knew from Alabama. Or Texas. If they do, I just hope I see them first, so I can hide. I don't want anyone to see me like this.

I look in my hat, and I've only received a dollar and seventy-eight cents. It's one of those nights.

I pull out my lucky red dragon. I hold him up, squinting my eyes so that my vision blurs, and pretend he's walking down the street, stomping on people. I make a few growls and squish sounds. I'm certain I look like a crazy person. But feeling like a little boy again is one of the few things that still makes me smile. Then I remember where I am.

No one gives money to people whispering to themselves.

"Wish me luck tonight," I whisper to the toy. I slip him back inside my pocket, then recount the money in my hat. It's still one dollar and seventy-eight cents.

I'm about to give up when I look across the street at the gay bar. Just inside one of the windows, an older man is sitting alone with a drink. He's looking at me. No. Staring. He smiles, gives a little wave. I offer a slight smile. After a few seconds, I wave back.

When he comes out, I see he's wearing dress pants and nice button-up shirt. He has leather loafers on. I wonder why he's so dressed up. Maybe he came from work.

He looks both ways before crossing the street. Then he strolls over to me slowly. He's maybe sixty-five or seventy. Or eighty. I don't know. Creases line his face when he smiles. He has blue eyes. Kind eyes. He asks, "How are you?"

It takes me a full minute to register that he's speaking to me. I realize it's been days since anyone has said a word meant for my ears. I ask, "Me?"

He chuckles gently. "I'm Roger."

He extends his hand for me to shake. It's been even longer since someone willingly touched me. When I shake his hand, the first thing I notice is the softness and the warmth of his skin. It makes me want to cry. I didn't realize human contact had become so precious.

"Rex," I say.

"Nice to meet you, Rex. Are you hungry?"

I nod.

He says, "Let's get you something to eat."

———

When Roger asks for a table for two, the hostess looks behind him and sees me. She looks confused. She says, "I have a table outside."

She sits us in a corner away from the other patrons. Roger doesn't seem to mind. I don't either.

It feels like an eternity since I sat in a real restaurant, the kind with waiters and waitresses. The menu boasts, *"Best Southern Home Cookin' This Side of the Mason Dixon Line."* When the waiter brings us two waters and a basket of cornbread and biscuits, it takes all of my restraint not to shovel the bread into my mouth. Instead, I take a sip of the ice water, letting the cold slide down my throat. But once I'm drinking, I can't stop. I gulp it down until it's gone.

The waiter looks at me with unease. "What can I get y'all to drink?"

"Arnold Palmer for me," Roger says.

I say, "Same."

After the waiter's gone, I grab a piece of cornbread and break it in half. Chewing with my mouth full, I ask, "What's an Arnold Palmer?"

Roger chuckles again. "Sweet tea and tart lemonade."

"Oh," I say.

Roger unrolls his silverware and places the napkin in his lap. That's what I should have done before I started eating. Even more important, I should have washed my hands. I excuse myself to go to the bathroom. I rinse my fingers and palms, lather them with soap, then wash them again. Using wet paper towels, I wipe my face and neck and forearms. I use a few more to wipe under my armpits. Then I wash my hands again.

I come back, sit down, and politely place my napkin in my lap. "Sorry for being rude earlier."

"Nothing to apologize for," he says. "No harm, no foul." Roger looks at me, and he smiles again. He takes out a pair of reading glasses, then picks up his menu. "This place is quite good. Everything on the menu is fantastic. You really can't go wrong. And it's my treat."

"Are you sure?" I ask.

"Of course," he says. "Order whatever you want. It's on me."

I look at the menu for a minute. But I can't help myself. I ask, "Why?"

Roger shrugs. "Why not?"

When the waiter returns, I order the catfish. It comes with green beans, fries, and hush puppies. I haven't had hush puppies since the last time I ate at a Long John Silver's, which was probably in high school. High school seems like another life. Someone else's life.

Roger orders a filet mignon. It comes with mashed potatoes, carrots, and gravy. I can't help but notice the prices. What Roger is paying for dinner, I could live off of for a month. But I don't say that. I don't say anything. I'm not sure what to say. So I let Roger start.

"So what's your story, Rex?" Roger asks. "If you don't mind my asking."

"No. I mean, not at all. Um . . . my story? I guess, I don't know. What do you want to know? Specifically, I mean."

"Where are you from? What kind of music do you like? What's the last good movie you saw in a theater?"

"Last good movie. . . . um, probably *Titanic*. No, wait. *Dark City*. I'm really into sci-fi, fantasy, that sort of thing."

"I don't watch much of that stuff."

"Did you see *Contact* with Jodie Foster? That's a fantastic movie."

"No, I missed that one."

"How about *Men in Black*?"

"Nope. Afraid not."

Silence stretches out in front of us. Then I say, "I like all kinds of music. Except rap. And really honky-tonk country music. Reminds me of home."

"Where's home?"

The question rings heavy in my ears. I'm not sure how to answer it. So I think back to where I was born, where I grew up. "Texas."

"And what brought you here to New Orleans?"

I answer as honestly as I can without going into it. "Bad luck."

"Sorry to hear that," Roger says. "I'm from Georgia. Savannah, to be exact. Came here for work, oh, thirty-something years ago."

"What do you do?"

"Nothing now. I'm retired."

Again, an awkward silence. I feel bad. I want to make conversation, but I don't know what to say to a stranger. Especially someone so much older than me. I reach for a biscuit, split it open, and dab it with butter.

"What kind of movies do you like?" I ask.

He ruminates on the question. "I like older films, especially black-and-white ones. *It Happened One Night. His Girl Friday. Roman Holiday. All About Eve. Rebecca.*"

I haven't heard of any of these movies. He can tell. So he adds, "*Rebecca* is an Alfred Hitchcock movie."

"I know him. He did *Psycho*. And *The Birds*."

"Yes, he did," Roger says. "Do you have any favorite black-and-white movies?"

"Hmm. I liked *Psycho* a lot. Um, and *Night of the Living Dead*. I mean, that's actually not my favorite. But it's one of the first movies I saw when I was little, and it totally wigged me out. Zombies still terrify me. Oh, and I love *Seven Samurai*. Have you ever seen that one?"

"I don't believe I have."

"I think it came out in the 1950s. It's this awesome fighting movie about a town that hires seven samurai—that's where the title comes from, obviously—to protect them from this gang of bandits, but all they can afford to pay them is rice."

"Sounds interesting," Roger says. Though I'm pretty sure

he's not sure about that one until he says, "I'll have to check it out." Something in his tone makes me believe him.

"Oh yeah, and I grew up loving *Wizard of Oz*. I know it's mostly in color, but it starts in black-and-white. Does that count?"

"It certainly does. Excellent choice. Friend of Dorothy and all that."

"What does that mean?"

"You really are quite young, aren't you?" Roger notes without any judgment. "The actress who played Dorothy was named Judy Garland. She was something of a tragic figure, but she was also full of camp. She's quite the gay icon. Lots of homosexual men, especially of my age, identify with her."

"Huh. I didn't know that."

"So . . ." Roger pauses before asking, "Are you a friend of Dorothy?"

"Um, are you asking if I'm—"

"Gay."

My face must seem hesitant, cause Roger suddenly looks as if he made a mistake. "You were sitting across from that bar, but I shouldn't have assumed—"

"No, it's okay. Yeah, I think so. I mean, I am. Mostly, I guess." That's the most honest answer I can give.

"Have you ever been with a . . ." Roger looks around. "A man before?"

Russell comes to mind. I look down at the table. "Yeah."

"Didn't end well?"

"It really didn't," I whisper.

"I'm sorry to hear that," Roger says. "I had my heart broken too. But I guess that was karma. After all, I broke my wife's heart when I came out and divorced her."

"You were married to a woman?"

"For nearly four decades. She was my high school sweetheart."

"But I thought you were—"

"I am. But back then it wasn't an option. I couldn't come out. I had to live a normal life. I married, I had kids, I had the white picket fence. But it's not what I wanted."

"What'd you want?"

Roger smiles at me. "I wanted it all."

"Did you get it?"

"For a time. But it . . . it didn't work out. We were from two different worlds, he and I. And now . . ."

"Now, what?"

"Nothing," Roger says. The kindness in his eyes gives way to a deep sadness. One that I realize was there the whole time.

The waiter brings our food. We eat. We go back to talking about movies. And music. And TV. Even though Roger hasn't heard much of what I reference, he seems to appreciate the commentary. When we're done with the main course, Roger orders dessert. Banana pudding.

When the waiter puts down the bill, Roger picks it up.

"Wow," I say, licking my spoon. "That was amazing. Every bite. Thank you."

"My pleasure," Roger says, putting down his credit card on top of the check. The waiter picks it up and disappears inside the restaurant.

Roger interlocks his fingers and rests his chin on his hands. He looks at me for a long time.

I ask, "What?"

"If you don't mind my saying so, you are a very handsome young man."

And I get this sinking feeling. Like I know what this evening was really about the whole time. I think of Russell. Him saying I owed him. Now I wonder if I owe Roger.

"Charming too," Roger adds. "Most young people can't carry much of a conversation. I get it. There's not much overlap between our generations to discuss. But you manage quite well."

"Well, I was rusty at first. It's been a while since I talked to anybody," I admit. "But talking is like dancing. It takes both people to make it work."

"Guess you're wise too."

"I have my moments."

Roger keeps staring at me. The waiter brings back the bill and his credit card, thanks Roger, and disappears again, leaving us alone. Roger adds the tip, signs, places the pen in the tray. He gazes at me.

He says, "So . . ."

I say, "So . . ."

"This is the part where I have to be completely honest or I miss my chance. Do you mind if I'm frank?"

"I thought your name was Roger."

Roger chuckles. "Funny too. You have everything going for you."

I look at my backpack and duffel bag under the table. "Hardly. Everything I own is in these two bags."

"Do you have a place to sleep tonight?"

"No."

"Would you like to?" Roger asks.

I'm not sure what to say. So I don't say anything. I look at my hands. Roger is nice. Really nice. And I actually enjoyed talking with him. But I don't want to sleep with him. I'm not attracted to him.

"Let me be clear," Roger continues. "I'm not asking for sex. Not necessarily. Unless you . . . I just . . . I wouldn't mind some company."

Roger can't look at me anymore. Now he's looking at the table. A gulf spills out between us. And I feel bad. I shouldn't have accepted dinner. I shouldn't have come along.

Roger says, "When you get to be my age, when you're a homosexual man, if you don't have a partner, or friends, or family, because you wasted your life pretending to be something you're not, you end up alone."

I remember all the stuff my dad said. I feel sick. I can't help thinking, He was right. My dad was fucking right.

My heart is breaking for Roger.

But it's also breaking for me. I'm looking at my future.

I notice Roger's hands. The veins just beneath the surface. The soft skin. The manicured nails trying to hide their age. These hands have lived a lifetime. And now . . . now he's just as desperate as I am. We're just desperate for different things.

"You could come over. Have a long hot shower. Or a bath. I could wash your clothes. You can sleep in a clean bed. I can give you money—"

"I don't want money," I say.

"I'm sorry, I shouldn't have—"

"It's okay," I say. "Dinner was enough. It was very kind of you."

He smiles. I smile back.

We sit there for a time. In silence.

Until, finally, I say, "I'll come over."

darker

Bourbon Street is bustling. The crowd is thicker, louder, rowdier. Tourists look like clumsy soldiers, replacing their rifles with long plastic cups full of margaritas, hurricanes, and piña coladas. Proud to wear plastic beads around their necks like jeweled necklaces meant for royalty. Their laughter and smiles are contagious. That's why I come here. Hoping I'll be infected by some kind of joy.

Cause, lately?

Lately, the nights weigh heavier on me. Like the sky is pressing down on me, crushing my rib cage, pushing air out of my lungs, making every breath more difficult than the last. Even the streetlights seem dimmer, so that they can't keep the ink-colored clouds from coming down, lying on top of me like a monster sucking out my spirit through my mouth. It's not real, but it seems real. It feels real.

It causes my thoughts to spiral again, only farther down.

I'm unable to keep them at bay, and demons overwhelm me with visions of all my tomorrows. Of trying to find my next meal. Of trying to get a job. Of going back to school. Of trying to get off the streets. Of what the rest of my days will look like if I can't. Of never having a family again. Of getting sick. Of getting addicted to drugs. Of being alone. Of being attacked. Or murdered.

And all the roads, all of those paths of thought, lead to one place: my death.

Maybe I will see it coming. Maybe it will be abrupt. Maybe it will hurt, and I'll be in pain, for hours, or days, dying of sickness, with no place to go. Or maybe it won't feel like anything. Maybe I'll just stop breathing in my sleep. And my body will lie undisturbed, swelling with maggots and decay. When the authorities finally find my body, they'll try to figure out who to call. They'll eventually track down my dad's number. Mona and Rebecca will crumble. My dad won't feel a thing. He'll be numb. He'll think this was what I had coming.

Or maybe he'll fall apart. Guilt will overcome him. He could have avoided this, if only he had loved me enough to keep me.

I'm not sure which scenario I prefer.

And what comes after? Is it possible I'll get into heaven—if there is such a paradise? Cause if there is, then that means I'm more likely to end up in a fiery inferno of punishment for my blasphemous actions.

Or, maybe, worse, I'll go the way of science, and I'll simply cease to be.

I try to imagine just not existing anymore.

My whole body lights up with agony. It's both physical and

mental. An internal pain that feels bigger than my body. Heart racing. Forehead sweating. Electricity running up and down my arms and into my legs. I wonder if I'm about to have a seizure. If this is it.

I don't want to die.

But I don't want to suffer anymore either.

And I'm suffering.

God, am I suffering.

I thought life was a struggle before. Trying to make friends. Trying to save money. Working to make good enough grades to get into college. To work hard toward a future. To find a job. To fall in love. To grow old, happy. But they were struggles that everybody shared. I wasn't alone, falling down a crevice in my mind, and the deeper I go, the harder it's going to be to climb out. If I even have the strength to pull myself out of this abyss.

I don't know what to do.

I don't know what to do.

I don't know what to do.

Everything hurts so bad. I can't breathe. My vision narrows. I feel like I'm having a heart attack. Like I'm going to die.

I'm going to die.

I'm going to die.

I'm dying.

I try to catch my breath. My lungs stutter. But I slow it down, inhaling and exhaling, trying to remember what calm felt like. Finally, the pain seems to recede. Not a lot, but a little. Enough that the pounding in my chest lessens. So I keep breathing. I keep breathing. I keep breathing.

Eventually, I pull the lucky dragon from my pocket. And I hold it. I feel its shape, pressed into my hands, anchoring me to my body. And I begin to pray to it. To pray to this ridiculous toy. I pray that I will be okay. That somehow I'll survive.

But right now?

I just don't see any way of that happening.

donuts

This late at night, most businesses are closed already. Windows reveal dark interiors, employees having gone home. But at the end of the block, bright yellow neon letters beam over a small shop. THE DONUT PALACE. Inside, a lone man picks up a long metal sheet covered with brown wax paper and half a dozen donuts. He empties them into a large clear plastic bag, already smeared with the glaze of other discarded donuts and apple fritters.

Hunger rips through me.

Is he tossing them out?

My eyes follow the bag as the worker walks toward a back room. I run around the side of the brick building, toward the alley behind. When I get there, the door opens, and the man tosses the plastic bag into a dumpster without a thought. The door closes behind him.

I move quickly, ready to dive in and rescue the pastries, when a haggard woman steps out of the shadows. Seeing me, she waves a cane in the air threateningly, snapping, "They're mine!"

Without taking her eyes off me, she stands on her tiptoes and fishes her arm into the dumpster to retrieve the clear bag full of cooked dough circles. She hisses, as though she might frighten away a cat, sending it scurrying away. But I'm not a cat. I don't move.

I could step forward and take the bag from her. A few slaps from a cane would be worth the prize. I could definitely take her. She's old. Her bones look frail. Her skin sags. But her eyes look wild. Desperate.

I suspect mine do too.

I push away some awful instinct to fight her. Deep down, I don't want to hurt her. Or anyone else. I hold my hands up in surrender. I say, "You have a whole bag. You can't eat all of them."

"How do you know?" she asks.

"I suspect."

"Yeah, well, you don't know shit."

She hikes the bag up over her shoulder and starts backing away. Pointing her cane at me, she says, "I'll scream, you come near me."

"I'm not," I say. "I'm not moving. Please. Just a couple."

She hesitates.

I wonder if she has kids. If she has family. Or *had*. What happened to her to bring her here? To the place where we both are? Scrounging for meals out of dumpsters?

"You have like twenty donuts in there," I say. "Please. Just a few."

She looks behind her. The alley runs behind four stores. It's dark. She realizes she couldn't escape me if I ran after her. The look in her eye? It's happened before. She doesn't want a fight. Neither do I. But I press my advantage. I stand up straighter.

"I'll give you one," she says.

"Four," I say.

"Two," she says.

"Three."

There's a pause. She considers.

"Three and you'll leave me alone?"

I nod.

She unknots the bag, reaches in. I imagine her dirty, grubby hands, and I'm about to protest. But I'm too hungry. I take a step forward, and she waves her cane at me. "I can do it," she growls.

She hands me a glazed donut. I devour it while she fishes out the second. An old-fashioned. I take a huge bite, my mouth still full. I realize I'm dropping precious crumbs all over the alley floor, and I force myself to slow, to take a second to chew, to swallow. The donuts are stale. Hard. I don't care.

Her hand brings me a third donut, and it's covered with pink frosting. I take it. I have a donut and a half, and I feel rich. A pauper no more. It feels like a feast.

She eyes me with curiosity as I chew. The stale donut finally goes down my dry throat, and I'm suddenly craving milk.

"Why do they throw them out?" I ask.

"No one wants two-day-old donuts," she says.

"They throw them out every night?"

"Every other. Only if there's some left over."

I take another bite of the old-fashioned. It's the best thing I've ever tasted.

"Don't get any ideas," she says. "This is my spot."

"Huh?"

"This is where I come. You want food thrown out? Find your own spot. They're all over the city."

"How do you find them?"

She laughs. "You look hard enough, you'll find them."

Wobbling, she staggers off. Her frame becomes a black silhouette in the alley, eventually emerging into the light at the other end, using her cane to step and step and step until she's gone.

rain

One drop. Then another. They hit my cheeks and ribbon down. I'm half asleep and dreaming, not sure if it's real or not. I hear thunder. The sound of a downpour racing my way. I grab my bags and make a run for it.

I turn down one street and then another, looking for cover, as the water starts to pelt me. Only a few blocks away, a bridge rises above the buildings. I make a beeline for it. By the time I get there, others are running for it too. Other people with no shelter.

We all awkwardly gather. Some shake water off their clothes, hats, jackets, even a broken umbrella. No one says anything. Instead, people look about, finding new places to rest, to settle in for the night.

One woman pets a black kitten she has in her purse. One man smells like he shit himself. The stink is unbearable. To get away, I meander through the maze of bodies, careful not to step on an outstretched hand or foot. I navigate around a tent, as well as several carts, one piled high with garbage bags, like a flock of black balloons bound together and grounded. I make my way to the other side, where a girl is sitting, smoking a cigarette.

She wears tattered denim jeans, a black Pantera shirt, and a leather jacket. Her hair must have been dyed blond months ago, but the roots have grown out, leaving an unsteady transformation from brown to white-yellow. She reminds me of a high school friend. Nicole, who always wore black and got me to listen to the Smiths.

I've seen a lot of people without homes, but most of them are middle-aged. Or older. This girl is my age.

"What are you looking at?" she snaps.

"Huh?"

"You're staring at me."

"I wasn't. . . . I mean, I was, but . . ."

"Spit it out."

"You're my age."

"Yeah, and . . . ?"

"I just . . . I haven't seen you around before."

"Well, you're seeing me now."

"Sorry for staring."

Someone in the distance hisses, "Shhhhhh."

I stand there awkwardly, looking for a place to lie down. The girl rolls her eyes, then scoots over. "Here," she says, nodding to the concrete next to her.

I sit. "Thanks."

Another long silence stretches out before us. She continues to smoke her cigarette. I don't know what to say. Finally, she asks, "Where you from?"

"Alabama."

"Florida," she says, pointing her thumb at her chest. "Why'd you get kicked out?"

"How did you—"

A little laugh escapes her. "Cause no one chooses to live like this." She takes a drag from her cigarette. "If you can call this living." She blows gently and a ring of smoke comes out of her mouth. It floats in the air, then dissolves away like a ghost.

I don't know how to answer. I don't even know this girl.

"Well?" she asks. "Don't be shy. We all got shit on or we wouldn't be here. What's your story?"

I say, "My dad kicked me out."

"Why?"

"For being gay."

She taps her cigarette and ashes float to the ground. After a minute, she says, "My mom kicked me out for getting pregnant."

Instinctually, I look at her stomach. It's flat.

Her gaze drifts away from me, out toward the rain. "I lost it."

"I'm sorry."

We sit in silence, until her stomach growls. "Any chance you have any food?"

I'm about to lie. But somehow that feels wrong. Like I'd be lying to Nicole. Instead, I reach into my backpack and offer her a half-eaten banana, still wrapped in its peel.

"Sorry. There's not more."

"You apologize too much."

"Sorry."

She laughs. As she pulls back the banana peel, she takes a bite, and then another. Chewing with her mouth full, she says, "I'm Sydney."

"Rex."

She shakes my hand.

Someone shouts, "Can't you see I'm trying to sleep? Shut up."

Sydney shouts back, "Why don't you fuck off?" She shakes her head. Then lowers her voice, muttering, "Stupid motherfucker."

Sydney reaches into her pocket and retrieves a cigarette box. She tips it into her hand, and a dozen half-smoked cigarettes fall out. "People are always throwing out good cigs. Waste for them, win for me." She offers me one with lipstick staining the end. "You want a smoke?"

"No, thanks."

"More for me," she says, using the first one to light the second.

"How long have you been—"

"On the streets? A while. Maybe two years? First in Orlando. Then started dating this guy, and we made our way out here to stay with his cousin. But she kicked us out."

"Where's your boyfriend?"

"Dead. Overdosed."

"Oh shit. I'm sorry."

"It is what it is," she says.

I think of Kurt Vonnegut's *Slaughterhouse-Five* and the protagonist who keeps saying, "So it goes," anytime someone dies. I recall an English teacher saying it was some kind of calm acceptance of the cruelty of life. I never thought I would miss high school as much as I do now.

"Why'd you come here?" she asks.

"A guy."

"What happened?"

I don't say anything. Instead, I look down between my legs.

She asks, "Forced himself on you?"

Ever so slightly, I nod.

"I've been there," she says. "Fucking men. They're monsters. Especially when it comes to that thing below the belt." Sydney points her cigarette at my crotch. "Hope you at least got some cash out of it."

"Cash?"

She shakes her head. "You're cute. You could earn some serious coin turning tricks."

"I don't know what you're saying."

"Trading a little nookie-nookie for cash money," Sydney says. "Best way to feed yourself out here. Don't tell me you haven't yet."

I think of Roger. But I never took any money. Still, I shake my head no.

"You will when you get desperate enough." Sydney takes a long drag from her cigarette. Holding the smoke in, she asks, "You don't have any relatives to crash with?"

"They're all too religious."

"Funny, that." She exhales a steady stream of smoke. "They're supposed to be the kind, compassionate ones, but they always end up judging and hating on everyone else."

"Not all of them," I say.

Sydney turns and lies down, putting her cigarette out on the damp sidewalk. "If you say so."

pancakes

W ake up," Sydney says, nudging me with her foot. "Let's go get breakfast."

I open my eyes. The rain's stopped and the sun is out. It's more humid than it has been in days, but I'm glad the water's stopped falling from the sky. I don't want to be trapped under the bridge or soaked to my skin.

Sydney stands over me, pulling out another half-used cigarette. She uses an old matchbook to light it. "Come on. I'm hungry."

"Where are we going to eat?"

"Trust me," she says. "I know places."

We follow people to a breakfast place boasting BEST PANCAKES IN THE CRESCENT CITY on a sign in front. As we pass the window, I see large stacks of pancakes on every plate, more than any one person can eat. There's a line of tourists waiting to get in on the left side.

"Park here," she says. We sit down on the right, just outside the window. Sydney pulls a deck of cards out of her leather jacket. She starts shuffling them.

"How do we get breakfast with those?" I ask.

"We don't. The cards are for us to play while we wait," she says. "The food will come. Know how to play Go Fish?"

We ask each other for cards while we wait. Every time a customer comes out, Sydney checks them over. The first one to come out with a bag of leftovers, Sydney asks, "Are you going to eat that?"

"What?"

"Are you going to eat that later, or just take it back to your hotel room and let it sit until you toss it out?"

"Oh, um, I . . ." The tourist looks at his partner, then hands over the bag. "I guess you need it more than I do."

"Darn tootin'." Sydney takes the bag. "Thanks."

As the tourists walk off, Sydney pulls the Styrofoam container out of the paper bag. She opens it and reveals half of a stack of four huge pancakes and a side of scrambled eggs. "Dig in," Sydney says. She picks up one of the halves and gobbles it down.

"How'd you do that?" I ask.

"What? I just asked for it," she says.

"Yeah, but you were so . . . so . . ."

"Aggressive? You gotta be."

"And everyone just gives it to you?"

"Not everyone," she says. "But there're spots you can count on. This place? The portions are huge. No one finishes their food. People either let the busboys toss it, or they decide to cart it around in case they get the munchies later. Lucky for us, most folks don't care that much. They know they can afford their next meal. Plus, you know, homeless guilt."

"Homeless guilt?"

"Yup. They feel bad for us. Especially when we make them notice us."

Twenty minutes and two games of Go Fish later, another pair comes out with a to-go bag. Sydney nudges me. "Give it a try."

"Um, excuse me," I stutter in a low voice. "Are you going to eat that later?"

Gruffly, the man says, "Probably."

"Well, if there's any chance you're not—"

"I am."

"Oh, okay."

I squeeze my lips together and look down, feeling like a failure. Then the wife takes the bag from her husband's hand and offers it to me. "Enjoy." As they walk off, she prods her husband. "You don't need to be a jerk about it."

"Not the way I'd go, but you did it," Sydney says. She takes the bag from me and opens up the box. "Jackpot! This place has great home fries."

hotel

old my purse," Sydney says. She looks both ways, like a spy not wanting to be seen. But it's nighttime and only a few people are wandering the side streets. She gets down on her hands and knees and crawls into a small opening behind some tall shrubs. When she returns, she's holding a large pink duffel bag.

"What's that?" I ask.

"My closet," she says.

"You don't carry it with you?"

"I don't want to lug it around all day in this heat. I like to travel light." She digs through the bag until she finds a sequin top. She holds it up and smiles.

Sydney nods for me to follow her to an alley, which she ducks into. She spins her finger downward in my direction and says, "Turn around. And keep watch."

A minute later, she comes out in a new outfit. The sequin

top and a short black skirt. She has on heels that *clip-clop* against the street. "Whatdya think?"

"You look great."

She takes a small bow. "Thank you very much." Then she looks me over, asking, "You have any clean clothes in your bag?"

"I have a cleaner shirt. It's a polo. And jeans."

"Put 'em on."

I go into the alley and change. When I come out, she says, "Much better." Then she takes my duffel bag, and her own, and returns to her hiding spot and stuffs our bags in there. "Give me your backpack too."

I don't move to take it off. This is everything I own. What if this is a trick? What if she's going to rob me? I say, "I can't."

She rolls her eyes. "Fine. I guess it makes you look like more of a tourist anyway." Then she takes my hand and drags me after her.

"Where are we going?"

A mischievous glint shines in her eyes as she pulls me along. "I want a drink."

————

We're standing across the street from a multi-story hotel. It's all brick and has open shutters on the sides of every window. Lights shine up from the ground, highlighting a blue flag with a white pelican on it. Guests walk in and out, some dressed up, some dressed down.

Sydney asks, "You ever come here?"

"No."

"Good. They won't know your face. Come on."

I grab her arm. "We can't just walk in there. They'll throw us out."

"Okay, look. When you walk in, act like you've been here a dozen times, like you're staying here for the weekend. But don't make eye contact with anyone who works here. Just follow me."

She starts to step off the curb, but I say, "Wait. What are we going to do in there?"

She rolls her eyes, getting frustrated. "First we're going to go to the bathroom and freshen up. Then we're going to the bar."

"We don't have any money."

"Don't worry about it. We'll figure it out."

She takes off. She's halfway across the street when I finally rush after her. When we walk in the doors, a blast of cold air washes over us. But my skin is still warmed by my own anxiety that we're going to get thrown out.

With conviction in her step, she strides forward, her heels *clip-clopping* on the marble floor. The check-in desk is far to the left side, the view mostly obstructed by several columns. Above us is a chandelier, giving off only the dimmest of light. At the far end are some carpeted stairs, but we don't make it that far as Sydney takes a right into a hallway.

At the end there is another turn, and then a set of bathrooms, men's and women's. Sydney gives me a wink and says, "Go clean up. I'll meet you at the bar."

"At the bar? In how long?"

"I don't know. Half an hour."

"Can't I just wait for you?"

"Yeah, that's not at all suspicious. Just wait for me on one of the chairs in the hallway. You have books in your bag, right? Read one of them, so you look natural."

Walking into the bathroom, I'm taken aback. The marble floor continues in here, and is matched by marble sinks with golden faucets. Instead of paper towels, they have actual cloth towels. There are several individual toilet stalls, each with a wooden door that goes all the way to the floor. As quick as I can, I grab four towels and soak them in water. Then I run into the handicap stall and lock the door.

I breathe a sigh of relief. This might be the cleanest bathroom I've ever been in. I kick off my shoes into the corner, then undress completely, careful to fold my clothes. Then I take my time wiping the wet towels over my entire body. The first towel is so soft, the cool wetness refreshing as I wipe off days of grime. I start with my face, then my neck, chest, stomach, arms, armpits. I take another wet towel and move over the lower half of my body, spending extra time on my crotch. Then, with the other two towels, I start over and do it again.

I let myself air-dry. The whole time I'm in the stall, no one comes in the bathroom. Finally, I put my underwear back on, and roll on my socks. It feels gross to dress again in already-worn clothes, but I don't have any other choice. When I'm completely dressed, I put on my backpack and tie my shoes. I pick up the wet towels, leave the stall, and throw them in a basket with other towels in it.

I wash my hands and face again.

Looking in the golden-framed mirror, I see that I don't look so bad. It's like night and day compared to my morning cleanups in the park public bathroom.

I'm reading *Interview with the Vampire* (for the fourth time this summer) when Sydney finally appears.

"Nothing like a clean bathroom, huh?" she asks.

"For real."

"Now, come on."

I trail down a corridor after her to two open doors. They lead into a dark bar, lit only by a few lamps designed to look like old lanterns. Chairs and couches are all upholstered in velvet or leather, and the tables in polished wood. The bar seats are mostly taken, and a dozen or so patrons are scattered around the rest of the space. Quiet lounge music plays from somewhere overhead.

Without hesitation, Sydney leads me to a booth in the back. She waits 'til I'm sitting and asks what I want to drink.

"A Coke?"

She shakes her head. "A vodka cranberry it is." She walks over to the bar and waits for the bartender to attend to her. She returns with two tall glasses, each filled with red liquid and topped with a circular lime. "Ta-da!"

"How are we going to pay for these?"

"We're not," she says, taking a sip through her straw. "Mike Johnson in Room 413 is going to."

"Who?"

"Guy at the bar. I overheard him tell the bartender when he paid his tab."

"So we're stealing from that guy?"

"Did you see his suit? His watch? He's loaded. And if he checks his bill later, he can always deny the charge. Then the hotel eats the cost. Look at this place, they can afford to buy us a few drinks."

"So we're scamming the place?"

"I prefer to think of myself as a con man. Or a con woman, I guess." She takes another sip from the straw. "Drink up."

I take a sip. The ice-cold drink runs down my throat, the bittersweet cranberry lingering on my tongue.

"What if we get caught?" I ask.

"They throw us out."

"They won't arrest us?"

Sydney shrugs. "Probably not."

"Probably?"

"Relax. Just enjoy it." Sydney picks out a cube of ice and crunches it in her mouth. "What was your favorite Saturday morning cartoon?"

"Huh?"

"When you were a kid. What did you watch?"

While I'm thinking back, I feel the alcohol start to warm my insides. "Smurfs. He-Man. Care Bears. My favorite was Dungeons and Dragons. I had a huge crush on this guy who could shoot energy arrows with his bow. I also liked this girl with red hair who had a cape that turned her invisible."

"Never saw that one," Sydney says. "Care Bears were cool. But She-Ra was a total badass."

"Yes! I loved her too. She was He-Man's cousin."

"Yup. And I was big into My Little Pony. I had to have all the figures. My dad used to buy them for me. One night he came home with this one, a So Soft Pony, named Cupcake. She was covered in light fuzz, like velvet, and she came with a comb and I spent hours brushing her hair. Man, she was like my most prized possession. I mean, she was until I discovered Barbie.

"Oh my god, I was such a girlie-girl. I had this all pink bedroom. Pink walls, pink sheets, pink clothes. My dad spoiled me rotten."

Sydney's eyes gloss over like she's reliving happy memories. She's smiling.

I like seeing her like this. So I don't say anything. Instead, I reflect on my childhood Saturdays, sitting cross-legged on the carpet, way too close to the TV, and eating Lucky Charms cereal, even though I didn't like the dry marshmallows. I preferred Cap'n Crunch.

Before I finish my drink, Sydney returns to the bar to get a second round. My head is starting to get floaty from drinking on an empty stomach, but I don't mind. Sydney is enjoying herself, and I'm trying to do the same. As I start to loosen up, so does my tongue.

"Why are you being so nice to me?" I ask.

Sydney shrugs. Takes another sip of her vodka cranberry. Then, playing with her lime, says, "You remind me of someone."

"Who?"

She squeezes the lime into her drink, then takes another pull from her straw. "My little brother."

"But you and me, we're the same age."

"You still remind me of him." She looks over at me. "You have the same eyes, all innocent and naïve. You kinda look like him too, especially the way you wear your backpack with both straps all tight. Plus, I'm pretty sure he was gay."

"When was the last time you saw him?"

"He was in the living room window, waving at me. Mom said she wanted to talk to me, take me out to eat, just mother-daughter time. So when we drove off, he was waving at me. I can't remember if I waved back. I don't think I did. Cause I thought I'd see him later."

Sydney starts tearing off pieces of her napkin. Her eyes get all distant, like she's looking past the table, past the floor, and into the earth.

"Mom took me out to this diner. It was next to a bus station. She was all quiet, the whole drive. I shoulda known something was up. When we got there, she didn't get out of the car. She said she knew. About the baby. That she and my dad weren't about to help me take care of it. She didn't scream or anything, she just talked at me in this real cold voice. Said Dad didn't want me around anymore. Said she was ashamed, that I was an embarrassment. That I disgusted her. She gave me some cash and told me to get on the bus and not to come back."

Sydney wipes her eyes one at a time. "She had to drag me out of the car screaming. But when she drove off, I just stood there. Eventually I got on a bus. And that was that."

After a deep breath, I say, "I'm so sorry."

Sydney takes the straw out of her glass and drops it on the table. She gulps down the last of her drink. Shakes her head, like she's trying to clear it. Then she closes her eyes, takes a deep breath. When she opens them, she says, "Another round?"

"Are you okay?" I ask.

"Nope," she says. Then she walks back to the bar.

jedi mind tricks

I always like this time of day," Sydney says. "When the sun sets, it's like the sky is all like those paints you mix with water. Watercolors, right? Then they catch fire, the light bounces off the buildings, and everything has this kind of glow about it."

She takes another drag off a cigarette.

"It is pretty," I say.

"Come on."

"Where we going?"

"Bourbon Street." She inhales, burning the white paper and tobacco down to the filter. Then she flicks it into the air. "I like the French Quarter. It feels safe here. Or at least familiar, I guess. And being around the tourists? Makes me feel like a tourist. Like maybe any day now I'll wake up and it'll be time to go home."

She exhales.

"I know, it's stupid."

"No, it isn't," I say. "I know the feeling."

"Doesn't hurt that tourists are more willing than locals to shell out a few quarters or dollar bills for us needy."

"Yeah, I figured that out the hard way."

"Yo, Sydney," someone says behind us. We both turn, and Sydney's face flushes with excitement at the sight of two guys. She runs over and leaps up, wrapping her legs around the taller one. They start making out. For a moment, a pang of jealousy runs through me. Like he might take Sydney away from me.

They're still kissing when the guy's hand moves up to grope Sydney's breast. She glances at me out of the corner of her eye and pushes his hand away. Like she would if I were her little brother watching. She steps down to the ground and brushes off her shorts.

"Rex, this is Dan. And that's Thomas."

Almost all of Dan's visible skin is covered in tattoos. Some look homemade. Like they were pushed in with ink from a sewing needle or a safety pin. I wince at the thought. He wears a wifebeater tank top and jeans. He has a Mohawk, and I wonder how he can afford a haircut, or if he does it himself. And if so, how? I can't remember the last haircut I got.

Thomas wears a black shirt that reads BLACK SABBATH, and has a fair amount of ink himself. His ears are pierced over and over, and a chain hangs from one earring, trailing to his nose ring. His greasy hair is long, just past his ears.

Both guys are in their early twenties. But it's hard to know how old someone is out here. Their eyes always seem older.

Dan gives me a once-over, like I'm a dog he wants to kick.

"The fuck you looking at?" Dan asks when he sees me staring at a tattoo on his forehead that reads ASSHOLE.

"Nothing," I say.

Dan shoves me and says, "You fucking my girl?"

Sydney shoves Thomas back. "He's a fag, stupid."

I hate that word, but I don't say anything to defend myself. For the first time, my queerness is a shield that protects me.

"Oh," Dan says, letting up a little. "Well, keep your hands away from me. I don't want AIDS."

"Real mature," Sydney says. She puts her arm in mine. "Rex here doesn't know shit. We need to teach him."

"Teach him what?"

"How to feed himself."

"Go suck some dicks," Dan says.

"Or let someone suck yours," Thomas says. There's no judgment in his tone or his body language. He shrugs. "Cash is cash."

"No, I'm talking about using the Force," Sydney says.

"The Force?" I ask. "As in *Star Wars*?"

"Jedi mind tricks, motherfucker," Dan says. He smiles. "Fine, you wanna learn, I'll teach you. But I get fifty percent of your take tonight."

———

Tourists flood the street. We're sitting on the curb outside a restaurant. "Got any change?" Dan asks, though it's more of a command than a question.

Customers go in and out of the Tex-Mex place. When they see us, some shrug. Some pat their pockets and say, "Sorry." And some—most—just ignore us. We're invisible.

Sitting this close to a restaurant, the smell of food wafting out through the open windows? It's torture. Skipping lunch makes breakfast seem like days ago.

A couple comes out, the woman holding a white Styrofoam box. Dan nods at her, saying, "I'm hungry."

She smiles as she hands him the box. She says, "Praise Jesus."

Dan grabs his crotch. "Praise this."

The husband pulls the appalled woman away, disappearing into the crowd.

"Score," Dan says. He opens the Styrofoam box, and my mouth waters at the contents. A half-eaten burrito, rice, and beans. He grabs a huge bite of the tortilla-wrapped chicken, and tucks it back in the box. "Let's go, freshman," he says to me, chewing with a full mouth. Thomas follows us.

Sydney doesn't move. I hesitate, but Sydney says, "I'm waiting for the next to-go meal. Go on."

"Your to-go box is open," I note to Dan.

"Yeah, no shit," he says. "That's on purpose. Now, shut up, watch, and learn."

He moves into the crowd, scanning. He pinpoints a man with a tourist shirt who is drinking from one of the oversized neon plastic cups. Dan walks right up to the man and slams into him. The Styrofoam box hits the pavement, the food spilling out into a small hill of what could have been in my stomach.

"What the fuck, man?" Dan shouts at the tourist. "You spilled my dinner!"

"Huh?" the man says, shaking his head as if waking up. "I didn't—"

"You ran into me and knocked the food right out of my fucking hand."

"I'm sorry," the man stutters. "Sorry."

"Sorry don't fix shit. You need to pay for my dinner."

"What?"

"That was twenty dollars," Dan growls, jamming his pointed finger into the man's face, just an inch away from between his eyes. "You owe me, man." Thomas backs up Dan, flanking the tourist.

The tourist's wife looks afraid. Dan and Thomas's tattoos don't help put her at ease. "We don't want any trouble."

"Then pay up," Dan all but shouts.

The tourist fumbles with his wallet. He pulls out a five and hands it over.

Dan snaps, "Five? This meal cost me twenty!"

The tourist looks at the burrito. "Yeah, but you already ate half of it."

"Don't tell me what I ate."

The tourist fishes out a ten. "I'm sorry, okay? That's all I got."

"Come on, Harold," the wife says.

They shuffle off into the crowd as Dan shouts after them, "You better walk away. Rude motherfuckers, this is my town."

Then Dan turns back to me, holding up his hard-won cash. "Fifteen dollars. I can buy whatever I want for dinner instead of begging for food. And the best part?"

He squats down, picks up the Styrofoam box, and uses his fingers to shovel the rice and half-burrito back into the box. "I can do it again with the same props."

He and Thomas smile.

"Jedi mind trick," Dan says, "is tricking people into thinking what you want them to think."

———

Dan fishes into his pocket. He reveals a pair of glasses. He waves them around like a magician. "Voilà!"

"They're broken," I say, noting the glass in one eye is shattered.

"No shit," he says. "I broke them on purpose after I lifted them from a pharmacy. They're reading glasses. Worth about ten bucks. If that. But for me, they're my number two moneymaker."

He moves into the crowd again. Thomas stays behind with me. He says, "Always look for a tourist. Not a young one, but someone in their thirties or forties. Not a strong one or a tall one. Someone medium size, or shorter than you. Someone you can intimidate. Look for someone not in a group. Usually a couple, or someone alone. Get them when they're vulnerable."

Dan moves through the throngs of people. When he finds his mark, he pounces. Only it's less of a leap, and more of a shoulder-slam. It all happens so fast, the victim doesn't see Dan toss the glasses at the pavement on purpose.

"The fuck?" Dan shouts.

The lone man turns. "What?"

Dan picks up the glasses. "You broke my glasses."

"No, I didn't," the man slurs.

"You slammed into me, then you stepped on them."

The man shakes his head. "I didn't."

"You did," Dan snaps. "You broke my fucking glasses. And you're going to pay for them. They cost me two hundred dollars."

The man looks confused. He looks at the glasses. He's doubting himself now.

Dan holds up the broken specs. "Fuck, man. I can't see shit with these now. You owe me a new pair."

The lone man's face looks frightened. Until his six friends

show up. The crew of men move around his sides protectively. They're both taller and stronger. "What's going on?" one of them says.

"Your amigo broke my glasses," Dan says.

"So?" the friend says. "Shit happens."

"Shit happens? Shit happens?" Dan growls. "I need my glasses, man."

The men talk among themselves, consulting each other. Dan's eyes count the men, and some of the conviction melts out of his stance. "Sorry," the tallest friend says. He nudges the victim to keep walking. They walk away as a group.

Dan hesitates, then grabs his target by the back of his shirt. "You broke my glasses. You gonna make me call the police?"

"Call the police," the friend says, speaking for the mark. The others step forward. They aren't playing anymore. And they look pissed at Dan for wasting their time.

"Look. Just give me twenty and we'll call it even."

The mark looks at the friend who first defended him, his eyes asking for direction. But the friend shakes his head no. "We're not giving you shit."

Dan puffs his chest out, proud peacock, saying, "Fuck you."

"Yeah, fuck you too," the man says. Then the men crowd around their friend and continue on their way.

"Fuck you!" Dan shouts after them. "Fuck you!"

Dan shoves the glasses in his pocket. He's all adrenaline. He slams past Thomas, and slams past me. "Fuck you two for just watching. You shoulda had my back."

Thomas shrugs. When Dan's far enough away, he says, "You win some, you lose some. And Dan hates to lose."

———

"You starting to get it?" Dan asks. He's counting his cash. I see enough tens that Dan could probably get a place to sleep. Or feed himself for a week. He crams the wad of bills into his pocket. Then he circles me. "Not that it's gonna work when you do it. You're about as intimidating as a kitten."

"Maybe that'll work to his advantage," Sydney says. "He looks trustworthy."

"Let's see you do it, then," Dan says.

I hesitate.

Dan shoves a mostly empty Styrofoam box into my hand. "Go on, then."

"I don't want to," I say.

"What do you mean, you don't want to? If you wanna eat, you have to."

"I don't mind just hanging outside a restaurant and taking leftovers," I say. "I don't want to steal from people."

"It's a dog-eat-dog world," Dan says. "If you think any of these pricks wouldn't do the same in our position, you're wrong."

I want to say it's not right. But I bite my tongue. The last thing I want to do is piss off the first group of potential friends I've encountered. Not when they're better at this than me. Living on the street, I mean. Not the scamming. Though they're obviously better at that too.

"You have one more Jedi mind trick to show off," Thomas says.

"It's a trick, all right, but nothing Jedi about it." Dan grins. He walks along the edge of the crowd, scanning for his next target.

This late at night, everyone on the street is drunk. I've seen it before. The slurring, the stumbling, the puking on the side of the road. This time, Dan picks a large, rotund guy. He bumps into him, gentler this time than when he did it earlier. In fact, he says, "Oh shit, man, I'm so sorry."

Then Dan parts ways. He walks over, a smirk stretched across his face.

"I don't get it," I say.

Dan holds up a wallet. "Idiot had his wallet hanging out of his back pocket. He was just begging for it to get stolen."

"You robbed him?" I say pointedly. "That isn't right."

"'That isn't right,'" Dan mocks, then laughs. He throws his arm around my neck, saying, "Look what we got, folks. Jiminy Cricket here is gonna be our conscience. Guide us to a life of virtue."

"That's not what I'm saying. But there're other ways."

"You've been on the street, what? A couple months? Less? Know how I know? Cause you're not hungry enough yet. When you are, when you really know what it's like to live like us, you'll do what you have to."

"You can go to the shelters. You can grab donuts behind donut shops. You can—"

"Beg? Plead for mercy? Ask god to take me back under his good graces?" Dan growls, his hands clasped together like he was some twisted angel. Then he gets in my face, yelling, "Fuck that. I'm done trying to be good. The world took everything away from me. Everything! It's my turn to take some of it back."

He storms back into the crowd.

———————

Sometime after midnight, I watch Dan and Thomas gorge themselves on fries and burgers, fresh and paid for with cash. Sydney eats from a leftover box she earned outside a restaurant. When she sees me gawking, she hands me what little is left.

"You want food, you got to earn it," Sydney says. "You can't just bum off the rest of us. We're in the same boat, remember?"

Dan throws a fry. It hits me in the head and bounces off onto the ground. I stare at it, wanting to pick it up and eat it, my pride battling hunger for control. I glare at Dan. He laughs. "Go on. You know you want to."

I say, "Fuck you."

"That's more like it," Dan says. "There's that fire inside. See? You and me, we're more alike than you want to believe."

"I am not."

"No," he says, "but you will be."

house

Thunder rumbles in the far distance of the night sky. Above me, the clouds have gathered into thick dark tufts that reflect the city lights. They're drifting down in a kind of fog, descending in a soft mist, promising a shower soon.

From the front of our small group, Dan says, "Looks like rain. I know a place we can crash. It's not far from here."

Thomas says, "Not at Stevie's."

Dan slaps him up the backside of his head. "You don't wanna come? You wanna sleep outside and get soaked? Be my guest."

"Who's Stevie?" I ask Sydney. She shrugs, she doesn't know.

"Don't worry about it," Dan says. "You're lucky I'm even letting you come along. Fucking sad puppy, following us around, begging for scraps."

I want to punch him in the face. Tell him to shut the fuck up. But I don't. I hate Dan. I hate him so fucking much. And I want to leave. But I want Sydney to go with me. And right now I don't think that's going to happen. So I guess I'm stuck. I tell myself it's better to be with people than be alone.

Dan leads the way, talking at Thomas, who doesn't say much. Sydney follows, smoking a cigarette, and I walk after her.

The neighborhood starts off lined with modest, well-kept houses. But a few streets later, the streetlamps grow farther apart and broken bottles litter the sidewalk, glass crunching under our feet. The lawns become less cared-for or forgotten altogether. One has a rusted swing set lying on its side. Another has an old truck, its tires having been taken away. I imagine eighty or a hundred years ago these places were new, full of loving families ready to start fresh in rooms waiting to be decorated with care. Now those dreams have fallen into ruin.

We walk block after block until we get to a lot. Standing in the middle is a battered house. Paint peels off its columns in thick strips, like bark from a dying tree. Its yard is covered in uneven grass and weeds growing wild. And a waist-high iron gate leans forward, a tall chain-link fence behind it. A sign reads STAY OUT. But beyond the darkness in the front, dim lights flicker from inside the windows behind the trees.

"This way," Dan says, leading us around to a part of the fence that's been cut away. While I'm crawling under, my backpack snags on the fence and I have to pull it free. A half-bricked path stops at a sagging porch. The boards creak, giving several inches beneath my weight, as if tired, ready to buckle and cave in. Without knocking, Dan opens the door and strolls inside.

The living room doesn't have light, except a faint glow from the next room. My eyes peer through the darkness at piles of newspapers, some plastered to the windows, as though wanting to hide this place from the outside world. On a two-legged sofa drooping against the floor on one end, someone smokes from a glass pipe. In a dining room, there's no table. Just a few bodies slumped against the joint where the floor meets the wall. Dead, or asleep, it's anyone's guess.

A rotting smell originates in the kitchen. Piles of mismatched dishes fill the sink and cover the countertops. An old table is littered above and below with pizza boxes, to-go bags, and Styrofoam containers. There's no sign of a trash bag or trash can. The only sign of care is the floral-print wallpaper, whispering from the past that this was once a happy place.

I follow the others up the stairs, forced to lunge over a missing step. At the top of the stairs, light creeps out from a room at the end of the hall. Plaster is coming off the wall in large abrupt pieces, revealing the wood beams and electrical wiring.

Dan leads us into a large room. There's no furniture except a small table in the far corner and a large lamp on the floor. The lamp looks naked without its shade. The light bulb is dim, casting long and tall shadows from every object in its path. Three people sit around. One of them is slumped against the wall, half-asleep, a goofy smile on his face. He looks younger than me. The other, a woman old enough to be his mother, sits scratching her legs, her arms, and her head over and over. She grits her yellow teeth, showing two are missing.

The third hops up with glee when he sees us. "Dan, my man!"

Crossing the room, he wraps his arms around Dan. He's shorter than Dan, but older, maybe thirty, thirty-five. He's wearing a trench coat, pants, and untied combat boots. He's not wearing a T-shirt, so we can see his belly button and a scar just above it.

"Stevie boy. How's it hanging?" Dan asks.

"Same old, same old," Stevie says. "I see you brought guests."

"Hope you don't mind."

"Not at all. The more the merrier," Stevie says.

Stevie nods to Thomas, who nods back. Then Stevie looks me over and says, "Fresh blood?"

"New to the neighborhood," Dan says.

"Welcome, welcome to my lovely home." Stevie waves his hand out with a flourish like he's presenting a palace of gold. "Mi casa es su casa."

I say, "Thanks."

Turning back to Dan, Stevie asks, "Are you here to crash or party?"

"A little of both," Dan says. "It's been a long week, and I'm feening for some fun."

"Most excellent." Stevie's grin vanishes when he kicks the shoeless woman, saying, "Out of the way, crackhead." She crawls to a standing position, her shadow contorting against the wall like a beaten animal, then rushes out of the room.

"Dan, no," Sydney says, touching his arm. "Let's just go to sleep."

He yanks his arm away. "Don't fucking tell me what to do."

"I'm not, I just, I don't want you to—"

"So don't."

Sydney steps back. Sliding down the wall, she crosses her legs, plops a cigarette into her mouth, and lights it. I sit next to her.

Stevie's shadow grows bigger and darker as he moves closer to the lamp. He reaches into his pocket and produces a handful of small white bags, knotted into little spheres. Inside some are little white rocks, in others, white powder. He asks, "Weapon of choice?"

"The usual. I'm looking for some bliss."

"Dope it is."

After Stevie and Dan haggle over price, they exchange drugs and money. Stevie nods Dan to the corner. On the small side table sits a couple of hypodermic needles, a spoon, and a lighter.

Dan takes a seat next to the lamp. He uncurls the plastic and fusses over the white powder, carefully placing it on the spoon. Stevie hands him the lighter. Dan flicks it on, the flame burning beneath the spoon.

"How about you?" Stevie asks.

"Nah," Thomas says. But he bites his lip.

Stevie's smile spreads across his face. "Are you sure? I think you want to. Last time, you were in heaven."

Thomas hesitates. He looks left to right, then up at the ceiling. He starts tapping his foot against the floor. "Shit, man. I wanna get clean."

"And then what?" Stevie asks, his voice dripping with honey. "You deserve a night off from the rest of the world."

Thomas's foot keeps tapping, more severe now.

"It's up to you," Stevie says. "I ain't forcing you to do nothing."

Thomas looks to Dan, who nods.

"Fuck. All right, yeah." Thomas reaches into his pocket. Pulls out a small wad of crumpled cash, smooths out the bills, and counts the money.

So only he can see, I shake my head, wanting to say, "Don't."

Thomas says, "Sometimes you just need to feel good."

Part of me wants to run, but my body is frozen. My limbs don't respond, except to grip my duffel bag even tighter. Lightning flashes outside the window. A second later, a huge boom of thunder sounds. Then the sky must have opened up, cause rain begins to pour down, thumping against the roof and the windows.

After Stevie deals to Thomas, he turns to me. "Will you be partaking this evening, young man?"

"Oh, um, sorry, I don't have any cash," I say as an excuse.

"First one's on the house," Stevie says with an inviting smirk, as if offering fresh-baked cookies.

"I'm good."

"Come on," Thomas says, slumping down next to me. "There's nothing like it. It'll make you feel better."

"No, thanks."

The white powder turns into boiling brown liquid on Dan's spoon. My nose burns with the reek of hot vinegar.

Dan catches my eye. "I see you," he says. "I know what you're thinking. So go ahead and think you're better than me. But when you've lived on the street as long as I have, you'll need some pleasure too. Whether it's heroin or fucking dudes or whatever gets your rocks off, you'll need it. You gotta have something to live for. Otherwise, what's the point?"

The needle inhales the dark liquid. Dan finger-thumps the upturned needle, squeezing out any air bubbles. Then he slides it into the crook of his arm, and squeezes down. In almost no time at all, a look of immense pleasure crawls across his face and his eyes roll back in his head. Thomas borrows the spoon and lighter.

"Let's go find another room," Sydney says. She stands, nodding for me to follow.

"You sure you don't want to stay?" Stevie asks. "You can party with me."

"Not my scene," Sydney says.

I follow her down the hallway, past one inhabited room, and into another. There's a single mattress on the far side, with no sheets or pillows, with someone sleeping on it. There're two makeshift pallets of cardboard, and a couple blankets on the floor.

"You sure you want to sleep here?" I'm not sure if I'm asking her or myself.

"Better than being outside," she says. Sydney takes the first pallet and lies down, using her purse as a pillow. I take the next. I keep my backpack on but use the duffel bag as a place to rest my head. I lay in the corner, with my back to the wall, so I can see the room.

I want to sleep, but I can't seem to close my eyes. My whole body is on high alert. Sweat starts to leak out of me. Knots from in my gut. My heart is in my throat, beating too quickly. I try to address the shortness of my breath, to take slower inhales, to exhale more slowly, to calm myself.

Inside, I'm all turmoil. A storm, ready to drown myself. Inside, I am crumbling. So I try to get outside of my thoughts. I try to survey my surroundings, to make shapes out of shadows. Sydney's form is a row of rising, gentle hills. The wood floor is an alien landscape. The patterned wallpaper is a set of faces, watching me.

With the window broken, the steady downpour echoes around the room. I recall all the times, being a little boy, sleeping under my *Star Wars* sheets, my window open, the rain outside lulling me to sleep with its natural rhythm. Everything felt so easy then. The only thing that scared me then was the monster under my bed. Now everything scares me.

———

I drift back and forth, between sleep and my cardboard pallet.

I dream of Russell's house, except it's empty. He's gone. All his furniture is gone. Even the fridge is empty. I walk down the shotgun hallway, and at the end is the back door. I step through, and I'm in my dad's house. It's empty too. I run from room to room, shouting, but no one is there. Outside, I run down the streets. There are no cars, and no people. And all the house doors are open and no one's inside any of them.

I feel like I can't breathe, and I crumple onto the sidewalk and start crying.

Then I hear screaming.

Real screaming.

And I'm awake.

The light flashes on in the room, a bright overhead light, and there's a man in the doorway. He has wild hair, a wilder beard, and his clothes are filthy. He has a knife and he's swinging it out in front of him, as if someone is there. He's screaming, "Leave me alone! Get out of my head!"

Sydney and I are both standing, backs against the wall. The other person who was sleeping in the room leaps off the mattress, runs into the closet, and slams the door closed.

The man with the knife continues to swing it, grunting and spitting. When he spots me, he bellows, "Why are you doing this?"

"I'm not doing anything," I say, holding my duffel bag in front of me like a shield. "I swear I'm not. You're okay. Everything's going to be okay."

"I'm not okay," he says, punching himself in the head repeatedly. "They're in my thoughts. They're getting everything.

Pulling it apart. Pulling it out." He remembers the knife and starts swinging again. Screaming, "Get out of my head! Get out of my head!!"

He lunges at me with the knife. I throw my duffel up. The knife sticks into it. I push with all my might, rushing forward, knocking the stranger onto his back. Then Sydney and I are racing down the stairs, out of the house, and into the rain.

We're blocks away when we see a bus-stop shelter. We run under the roof, to protect ourselves from the rain, even though we're already soaked. I lean forward, hands on my knees, trying to catch my breath. Sydney does the same.

Finally, I remember. "What about Dan and Thomas?"

"Fuck 'em," Sydney says.

shake on it

Last night was pretty fucked," Sydney says to me.

"It really was." I ask, "Does that kind of stuff happen a lot?"

"More than it should," she says. "I've seen some wild shit. There's always crazies. Especially when drugs are involved. I try to stay out of crack houses, but sometimes . . ." She starts biting her fingernail. "It's nice to have a roof over your head."

We're sitting outside of the pancake restaurant, the morning light peeking over the eastern buildings. Both of us have our signs leaned up against our legs, in case we can collect change while we wait for leftovers. So far, no one has come out with a to-go bag. It might be one of those days.

A pang of guilt rises up in me about Thomas. And Dan too, I guess. I hate him, but I don't want him dead. I ask Sydney, "Do you think Dan and Thomas are okay?"

"Who the fuck knows?" Sydney says, all hard. After a beat, she softens. "I hope so."

"Is Dan your boyfriend?"

"Depends on the day of the week." Sydney spits out part of a fingernail. "Not really. I mean, I enjoyed hanging with him sometimes. And, yeah, I thought he was a stud. I sure know how to pick my men, huh? Always assholes who love their drugs."

She's about to put her fingertip in her mouth, but stops herself. "Fuck, I hate when I'm out of cigarettes. I can't stop biting my nails."

"What if he got hurt?"

"Then he got hurt," Sydney snaps. "Nothing we can do about it now."

"But that guy with the knife—"

"Jesus, Rex, let it go."

"I'm sorry, I just—"

"I don't want to think about it, okay?" She puts her hand up between us, bites her lip, closes her eyes like she's wishing me away. She says, "I have to take care of myself. No matter what happens, I've gotta be priority number one."

"That seems so lonely."

"It is."

"Then how do you keep friends?"

"Friends?" Sydney laughs. "Out here, everybody's looking out for themselves. Most of 'em just waiting to stab you in the back. First chance they get, they'll steal your money, your clothes, your shoes . . ."

"You wouldn't do that."

Sydney shakes her head. "You don't know what I've done."

I say, "Then I wouldn't do that."

"Not yet, maybe," she says. "Give it time."

"No way. Not gonna happen. I won't let the streets turn me into . . . into . . ."

"An animal?" Sydney says. "All we do is scavenge for food and water and a place to sleep. We're chasing basic needs. Nothing else. If that's not an animal, I don't know what is."

————

All the change we earned this morning adds up to less than six dollars. We split it.

After, we walk awhile. Then we sit, tucked under a bridge, hiding from the sun. Bored, I pick up pebbles, set them on the edge of the decline, watching them start to tip, then tumble their way down the slanted concrete toward the stagnant water below.

"Guess tonight I have to work," Sydney says.

"Work?"

"Turn some tricks," she says.

"You don't have to do that."

"I do if I want to eat."

"So eat tomorrow."

"If I don't eat today, there's no guarantee I'll eat tomorrow. Then I'll be too weak to fight off someone if they wanna hurt me. I need my strength if I'm going to work. Better to earn money while I can than wait until I'm delirious from hunger."

"I'm coming with you, then," I say.

"It doesn't work that way. I can't have you hanging around in the background looking like my pimp."

"But you said it yourself, it's dangerous."

"Every day is dangerous," she says. "You just have to face it."

"Or avoid it."

Sydney looks me in the eye. "You're unbelievably stupid."

"I am not."

She shakes her head. "The streets will break you."

"Maybe they won't."

"Maybe," she says. She rummages around her purse, pulling out a paper cigarette box. It's still empty. "Fuck." She crushes the box in her hand and tosses it. She gets up, dusting off her butt. "I need to go get my clothes, clean up. See ya."

"That's it? You're just taking off? Am I going to see you again?"

"Probably," she says. "The city isn't that big."

"What if we meet again? On purpose, I mean," I say.

"What do you want from me?" she snaps.

"I just. . . . you're the first friend I've made out here. And I think . . . you and me should . . . should stick together. I'll pull my weight, and we'll get food and we can share. . . . and maybe we can find a way off the street. Get back on our feet. Make things better."

"We're not Disney princesses, Rex. We don't get a happily-ever-after."

"Maybe we do."

Sydney shakes her head. "You're sweet." Like it's a consolation prize, she kisses me on the cheek.

"Please don't go away." I'm trying not to cry. But I'm failing. "I don't want to be alone anymore."

"You already are," she says. "You just have to be okay with it."

"Why? Why do I have to be okay with it? Why can't we change it?" I grab her hand. "You don't have to be alone. We can take care of each other."

Now Sydney's eyes are welling up. She shakes her head, exhales heavily. After a minute, she says, "Fine."

"Really?"

"You fucking cross me, I'll kick your ass." Sydney offers me a half smile. "We can hang for another week or two. See how it goes. I'm not making any promises beyond that. Okay?"

"Shake on it?"

"You're so ridiculous." She reaches out and takes my hand. We shake.

"You sure I can't come with you?"

"I'm sure. But I'll meet you back here after. Don't wait up. It'll be late."

"I'll be here."

"I don't doubt it," Sydney says.

sunrise

I'm under the bridge, on a pile of cardboard, being lulled to sleep by the sounds of trucks and cars rushing by overhead. I wake up a few times in the night, but there's no sign of Sydney. Each time I come to, I'm a little more anxious.

As the sun comes up, I sit up, look around, hoping Sydney will have snuck over and fallen asleep beside me.

But there's no sign of her.

I reach into my backpack, pull out my little red dragon for luck. I rub him over and over, rocking back and forth, asking him to make her return.

today

It's been a week. I keep returning to the same bridge. Keep hoping she'll show up. I read there. I sleep there. Hoping she'll be there, waiting for me, when I wake up. But it doesn't happen. I see familiar faces. But not hers. Not Sydney's.

I gaze up at the graffiti, at the colorful tags of people who came before. Whether they were homeless, or in gangs, or just simply artists, I don't know. But for me, this is the closest I'll get to being in a museum anytime soon.

Standing up, I have to shake myself off. No matter where I sleep, or how much cardboard I put down, dirt and sediment gets everywhere. Like the freeway overhead dusts me gently in my sleep, not with the sleeping powder of the dream god Morpheus, but with grime, particles from tires that come from distant places.

Near the center of the underpass is an orange tent. A woman lives there by herself. Every morning, she comes out and sweeps the dirt and dust away from around her home. She wears a plastic bag pulled over her hair, and a flower-print housecoat that reminds me of an old woman from a cartoon. I wonder where she got the broom.

Someone honks. Maybe someone rushing to get to work. Maybe someone running errands. Maybe a parent taking their kids to school. I imagine bologna sandwiches in brown paper bags or Tupperware containers or lunch boxes, sitting in the passenger seats of their car or in a colorful backpack, to be ignored until later, when the food will be eaten without a second thought. My stomach rumbles.

After my morning routine, I walk to the Pancake House and take a seat near the entrance. Mostly the tourists in line for food ignore me. One of them offers me a look of annoyance. I wonder if I stink.

An hour goes by. A couple comes out. Without my asking, they offer me their to-go bag. I say, "Thank you."

But when I open the bag, I don't eat. There's a receipt on top of the Styrofoam container, with a date I recognize all too well. It's August 18.

It's my birthday.

I take the half-eaten short stack of blueberry pancakes across the street, to enjoy my meal out of the direct view of the patrons. Eating with one hand, I hold the receipt in the other, gazing at the date and trying to remember where I spent my last birthday.

In Texas, I know that much. Ready to enter my senior year of high school. That means I would have been in Abilene, living with my abuela. She made me an omelet for breakfast, then drove me to driver's ed class. After, she took me to Chik-fil-A for lunch. Later that night, she surprised me with cupcakes, made from a box mix.

The year before, I celebrated with friends. We went to Applebee's. Or was it TGI Fridays? I push my memory, but all I recall is us sitting around a table eating mozzarella cheese sticks and loaded potato skins and fried chicken tenders with honey mustard sauce.

I think back to other birthdays in the past. Sometimes there was a cake. Sometimes there was ice cream. Sometimes there was nothing. But even though I don't remember, I know I always crawled into my bed at the end of the night.

I try not to think about where I'll sleep tonight.

Instead, I focus on my food. With the last piece of pancake, I soak up every drop of syrup. I throw the container and the bag in a trash can. I put the receipt in my pocket next to my dragon.

Walking, I think of all the neighborhoods I've traveled through. Audubon Park, Freret, Touro, East Riverside, Irish Channel, Lower Garden District, Warehouse District, Storyville. Think of all the famous landmarks I've stood in front of. The French Quarter, Lafayette Cemetery, St. Louis Cathedral, Preservation Hall, Jackson Square, the Superdome. Where do I want to go on my special day?

I make my way down a street new to me. And then another. I want to get lost. And I do.

Then I find myself standing in front of a public library. My abuela always took me to libraries when I was a boy. Over summers, I spent hours there reading in beanbag chairs. Eventually, I stole away to my local library to escape from my home life. It was always a welcoming space. And the books . . .

I take a deep breath as I open the door, hoping no one will look at me, judge me. The receptionist has her head down, checking in books. But an old man reading a newspaper gives me a foul, condemning look, as though I've invaded his space. Which I suppose I have. Guilt rolls over me. But the air-conditioning is too much of a draw on a hot, humid day like this one.

Wandering the aisles, shelf after shelf after shelf, I find myself browsing the titles of books. So many books. So many that I read in my life. My life before.

Brave New World. Dune. The Hardy Boys series. *Alice in Wonderland. A Clockwork Orange. Wuthering Heights. The Great Gatsby. Tess of the d'Urbervilles. The Lion, the Witch and the Wardrobe. Great Expectations. The Adventures of Huckleberry Finn. Misery. The Catcher in the Rye. Frankenstein. The Odyssey. Charlie and the Chocolate Factory.*

So many memories come rushing back. It's a flood of nostalgia, for all the times I escaped into a book. And for a minute, a long minute, maybe a few, I consider stealing one. Just one book. There's so many.

But I don't.

Instead, I find a corner and cry.

––––––

The heat is unbearable. I find a tree in the park and lie under the outstretched limbs, thankful for the leaves. I take off my shirt, shoes, and socks, hoping some tiny breeze will dance across my skin. I lean against the tree and nap in an awake kind of way. Eyes closed, but aware of every sound, even as my thoughts drift like clouds.

Holding it in my hand, I rub the curves of my luck dragon. I'm not sure what I'm hopeful for. A cake? A cupcake? Maybe some half-eaten dessert? I'll pretend it has a candle in it and blow out the flame, make a wish, a wish to get off the streets, to find a home again.

I'm not greedy. I'd take a small studio with a tiny bathroom and a kitchenette. The fridge would be stocked with food, and I'd have a job to go to earn enough money to pay my bills and maybe eat out with friends once a month, or go to the movies.

As the sun sets, relief washes over me. I gulp down water from the park fountain, letting it fill my empty stomach, wondering what the weather is like here in the winter. Will it be cold, will it snow, will I freeze to death?

Walking toward the French Quarter, I go where it's busiest. Maybe I can scrounge together enough coins and dollars to treat myself to something special. A meal. Maybe I'll run into Sydney. Maybe I'll run into Roger, and he'll take me out to dinner again.

In front of a glass window, I stop. My reflection looks so much older. Grit stains me, my clothes, under my fingernails. I wear the street on me like a uniform that can only be earned by begging, eating out of trash cans, and sleeping on cardboard. I want to be disgusted with myself. But I'm too tired for even that.

The streets grow thick with throngs of people. Music and shouting fill the air. Beads, bars, neon signs, tall plastic cups, drunk tourists and locals alike. It seemed so magical when I first arrived. Now I take my seat against a wall, place my sign, and sit with my hat out in front of me.

I sit for an hour. The *clink-clink-clink* of coins joins the parade of noise. And I try to be grateful. Until—

A shoe crashes into my hat. Kicks it, and my change spills along the street, some coins spinning, falling flat, others fleeing away from me. I chase after them, as laughter hails me from above. After I've grabbed what quarters I can, I look up, saying, "What the fuck?"

Three stocky guys, only a few years older than me, stand

over me, wearing shirts with Greek symbols. Frat boys. Already I'm worried, but as they laugh, I can't bite my tongue. "You did that on purpose."

"What if I did?" asks one of them.

"Serves you right," another adds. "No one wants to see you. You're ruining our visual fun fest."

The third is staring off at a group of women, shouting, "Show us your tits!"

One of the women flips him off.

"Bitch," he says. Burps. Takes another swig of his beer, crushing the can on his forehead with a grunt.

The three of them walk away. I want desperately to shout after them. To call them out. To fight them in the street. But I'd only have my ass handed to me. And I don't want to risk it. Not today.

———

I walk away from Bourbon Street with enough money to buy myself two Happy Meals. But it's too late. McDonald's is closed. Still, my mouth waters at the thought of a McDonald's breakfast.

Turning down a side street, I make my way toward the park, hoping I'll get a night in the grass without police. Entering from the next block are three shadows. I cross the street, hoping to be invisible.

But as they get closer, they cross the street too. In dim light, I can see it's the frat brothers. I start to cross the street, but two of them do the same. The third walks around, flanking me.

"Well, what do we have here?"

"It's our friend from earlier."

"I wouldn't call him a friend."

The three of them laugh.

I try to walk away. But one of them pushes me. "Where ya going?" He stumbles and sways a little, drunk. All of them are drunk.

I say, "I don't want any trouble."

"Who wants trouble?" he says. "We just wanna have fun."

"Leave me alone."

I try to brush past, and another grabs me. He shoves me to the guy behind, who shoves me back, like a basketball being passed back and forth. "Fuck, man. He stinks. Don't make me touch him."

"He's probably filled with parasites."

"Diseased from eating rats and pigeons."

"AIDS from all those needles."

I am trying to get away. Again, they shove me back and forth.

"Just let me go," I say.

"Say please," one frat brother says.

Trying to will myself to say it, I fail. My pride gets in the way. Instead, I can't help it, I say, "Fuck off."

"What'd you say?"

"You think you can talk to us like that, you piece of shit?"

One shoves me from behind. Instead of getting shoved back by the brother I was shoved toward, he rears back and brings his fist forward, hitting me in the face. I taste blood, and I'm not sure if I bit my tongue or he busted my lip. Then I realize my nose is gushing.

One of them hits me in the side. Another hits me in the back. Then I'm on the pavement, and they're kicking me. One after the other, knocking the air out of my lungs. I can't breathe, and I can't stand. They're kicking my legs, kicking my arms, kicking my ribs.

I curl into a fetal position, the way I hid in my mother for nine months, hoping this protects me. Instead, the shoes keep coming. Until bright white takes over my vision and I feel like the world is closing in, smothering me. I'm going to pass out.

But the frat boys tire themselves out first.

"No, fuck you," the one says, exasperated. Then he spits on me. They all spit on me.

One last kick to the head.

They walk down the street, laughing, high-fiving.

I just lie there.

Broken.

the bridge

When I'm done crying. When I can breathe again. When I'm alone. I'm still waiting to get kicked. For a fist to find me. For more people to spit on me.

Despite the heat, I'm shaking.

My face is sticky with caked blood. I force myself to blink. I have both eyes, despite the ache that says otherwise.

I'm in and out of it, not sleep, but consciousness. Until a car is honking at me. I raise my arm to the headlights, trying to shield my eyes. I hope it's an ambulance, but it's just a cab. The driver doesn't bother to get out. He reverses the vehicle back into the adjoining street, then zips off.

It takes a while to pick myself up, to stand. I stumble along until I find a water hose behind a building, then wash myself. The water runs crimson until it doesn't. I take off my shirt, covered in blood, and rinse it. I hold the cold rag up to my face, and try not to cry.

I take out another shirt from my duffel bag, and when I lift my arm to put it on, an excruciating agony blossoms in my side, at the bottom of my rib cage. It feels like I'm being stabbed.

Eventually I place one foot in front of the other. I hobble, slowly, gently, unable to move as far or as fast as I usually can. Trudging along as the moon disappears and the sun rises over the city, it takes me hours to make it to the bridge. When I get there, the old woman in the housecoat is sweeping the asphalt outside her tent with the broom. She doesn't bother to look at me as I gather cardboard and lie down.

———

Under the shadow of the bridge, I try to sleep. Every time I move, there's pain. My face. My ribs. My arms and legs. I tell myself I'm not dying, but I'm not sure if I even believe that. It hurts to breathe, to swallow, to shift my weight. And every time I fall asleep, I jump awake, waiting to be attacked again.

I reach into my pocket to rub my luck dragon. But my pocket is empty. It was in there last night. I turn out my duffel bag, and then my backpack, looking for it. I check my pockets again and again. It's not here.

And I'm crying, cause all I can think is that it's out there somewhere, by itself, on the street. Alone.

Tourists won't see it underfoot and will trample it, crushing it. Or it's soaked in beer and vomit, to be washed down a drain. Or it's been swept away by the trucks that suck up the trash in the street, and it's off to some dump where it'll never be cherished again.

I'm moaning now, sobbing, tears streaming down my swollen face. I'm curled up into a ball, rocking back and forth. I desperately want someone to hold me. To pat my back and tell me it'll be okay. To kiss my forehead and assure me that was the worst of it.

But no one comes to comfort me.

Sydney was right. We're all on our own.

———

I walk into the black of night.

If I was invisible before, I'm even more so now. When someone looks at me, they avert their eyes, turn their faces away, walk more quickly. If they don't see me, then for them my pain doesn't exist. I don't exist.

This morning, I saw my reflection. Two black eyes, a swollen lip, bruises all over my body, a limp in my left leg. When I move, the pain in my side shoots through me like electricity.

I don't understand how I got here. I know how I got here, but I don't understand why. Why did my dad forsake me? Why did I have so much pride? Why didn't I beg to stay? Grovel to keep my place among the living?

Cause I don't feel like I'm living. Not anymore.

I'm here, but I'm not alive.

Not really.

I'm just a shade. A shadow of my former self.

I'll never get back to where I was. When I had friends. When I had a job. When I had a future. When I had a place in the world.

Instead of returning to the encampment under the bridge, I take the long way around, up onto the bridge. I walk the two-foot path on the side of the freeway as it inclines. Walking up, as though moving toward heaven, one slow step at a time, to a heaven I don't believe in. Cause if there's a heaven, there is a god, and how could such an all-powerful, all-seeing, all-loving being exist and let so much suffering go on down here on earth?

One foot in front of the other. I try to ignore what I'm doing. Why I'm coming up here. It's been in the back of my mind since I spent my birthday alone, since I got the shit kicked out of me, since my blood was pouring out of me onto the street. I don't want to admit it, I don't want to think it, but I'm just lying to myself if I don't.

I'm done.

I'm so done.

I'm tired of all the hurt.

A truck honks as it races by, its rush of air blowing me into a stone railing.

I've spent so much time under the bridge, but I've never been up here on top of it. I never noticed, but the structure is magnificent. It soars over the river, this engineering feat, a creation of man. Built to withstand the weather. Built to let hundreds of tons of commuters travel across it day and night. Built to bridge a gap. Like the gap that exists between me and the rest of the world.

When I reach the center of the bridge, I stare out over the water. Over the lights of the city. Over the world that doesn't want me.

I look over the edge, wondering if I'm high enough up. If my neck will snap when I hit the water below. Or if it's just going to hurt so bad that I can't swim and sink below the surface and drown. Or, if I survive the fall and the water, if I'll have enough strength to swim to shore.

I try not to think about what comes next.

And I climb the railing.

I stand on the edge.

I don't want this to be my life anymore.

I don't want to live like this.

I can't live like this.

It's too hard.

Too painful.

Too much.

The river moves below me. Flowing. Never-ending. In motion, moving toward the ocean. And I think of waves, crashing against the shore. Then I think back. To being a boy on the beach, the salt water curling around my toes in the sand. To cake, the soft sponge and the sweet icing. To the laughter of my friends in high school. To camping with my dad when I was little. To my mom dancing on Cinco de Mayo in a blue dress sewn with bright flowers. To Christmas morning with my abuela.

My mind wanders through thoughts of the past as I stare down at the night water coursing below, dark in its depths. I don't know what happens after you die, but I could find out right now.

It would only take a moment. I would fall for a few seconds. Then it'd be over. The pain would go away, the suffering would stop, all my problems solved.

So why am I hesitating?

Why can't I step forward?

———

Why?

———

And then I'm crying. Not a soft cry, like every cry I've known before. It's beyond sobbing. Beyond weeping. It's a furious howl that pours out of me, from deep inside, deeper than my heart, from my darkest depths. It is unleashed like a violent storm. And I'm screaming at the wind. Screaming into the sky. Screaming at the world.

Cause I'm not done.

Cause I can't imagine not existing.

Cause I don't want to leave this world. Not yet. Not like this.

———

So I crawl off the ledge.

I collapse on the side of the bridge. Lying on the narrow sidewalk, I feel it. Truly, really, feel it beneath me. The solid ground rising up to hold me. Gravity hugging me in place as the world spins. Like I do have a place. Right here. Right now.

And it's all so beautiful. Why did I want to give it up? Why did I want to give up? Why, when I have so much left to do?

I don't want to die.

I want to live.

phone call

The sun rises. I watch it from the bridge's summit where I sit. From the spot where I stepped back from the ledge. I haven't moved more than a few inches all night. I needed to wait, to see the light fight off the darkness.

It's a soft haze at first, just a dark blue coming over the horizon. But the deep cobalt warms until it's burning orange, and the sun, just a pinpoint of its crown, penetrates the line of land in the distance. The way a child comes into this world, the sun is born. Night fades into a soft blue, and there's not a cloud in the sky.

I get up, finally, and I start walking.

———

My pride has kept me here, I think. I could have reached out to someone. Asked for help from someone. Maybe someone from my past. From before Alabama. From my life in Texas. But I had so much doubt about who would love me, or just like me, this new version of me. This queer version.

I know who to call.

I walk until I see a pay phone. I don't have even a single quarter to my name. So I pick up the phone and dial zero.

"Operator, can I place a collect call?"

My stomach rumbles with hunger. With my face looking like a swollen pizza, I wonder if I could score a stack of pancakes.

"Yes! Yes, I'll accept the charges," her voice says from the other end of the line.

I melt just hearing her familiar accent. This time, my crying isn't violent. It's soft and gentle. As if from a wild animal that's lost all its rage. All its anger. All its hate. I'm exhausted, and I can't help but shed more tears at the tone of her soft, caring words.

"Rex?" my abuela says. "Rex, is that you?"

"Can you . . . can you send me twenty dollars?" I ask. "I'm sorry. I just . . . I just want to eat."

And I hear my grandmother crying on the other end. She says, "I've been trying to find you. But no one knew where you were."

"I'm in New Orleans. I'm alive," I say weakly, as if reassuring myself. "I came here, I tried to find work, but I couldn't, and then I didn't have a place to stay, and everything fell apart, and I haven't eaten a real meal in days, and . . ."

I can't tell her what I've done to survive. I'm not ready. The silence stretches out into tears from both ends of the public pay phone.

"Shhhh," she says. "Time to come home."

Home. That word is so loaded. So heavy now. I took it for granted before. Now it means so much. But is it real, or just a lie?

"I will wire you three hundred dollars," she says. "Find a hotel, take a shower, eat, and sleep. In the morning, come back to Abilene."

I don't know what to say. I think of her house: 1214 South Jackson Drive, Abilene, Texas. I know the layout like the back of my hand. The red bricks, the white-painted wood out front. The inside, smelling of pine. She keeps her house so clean, and her fridge full. Anytime I visited, she would have fresh lemonade waiting for me, and chicken spaghetti. And so many hugs.

I don't want to burden her. I don't want religion to come between us when she finds out why I'm here. But . . .

"Please, mijo," she whispers into the phone. "Por favor. Come home."

the last night

I go to Western Union and show them my ID. They hand me cash, crisp twenties, weighing heavy in my hands, one after the other, adding up to three hundred dollars. After putting the money in my wallet, I shove my wallet into my front pocket, holding my hand over it. I try to avoid eye contact with anyone, fearing someone will know, and rob me.

But it's daylight, and no one would suspect I have any money. Not looking like this.

The first thing I do is eat. I duck into a Popeye's and get a fried chicken platter with fries and a biscuit. I try to eat it slowly so I don't make myself sick. The Coca-Cola helps settle my stomach, which is crammed with too much food for how small it's become. I refill my cup twice. Then I take the cup with me, eating the ice until it's melted into water.

It's a long walk to Walmart. The whole way, I'm thinking, It's already gone. My truck was probably towed. Then I'll have to find a bus station. But that's fine. It won't stop me from getting back to Abilene. It'll just take me longer.

But when I approach the back of the superstore's parking lot, overwhelming relief washes through me. Like air is filling my lungs for the first time. My truck is still sitting there, hiding among the employee vehicles.

I fumble the keys out of my backpack. When I open the door, a blast of heat punches me in the face. But the smell is the same.

I drive on fumes to the first gas station I see, and fill up the tank. It's hard to hand the money to the cashier, but the fuel is going to get me to Abuela, to a roof over my head. Deep down, I'm still worried that she'll ask why my dad kicked me out. If me being gay is a problem for her. If it is, will she boot me out too?

But I can't think about that. Not yet. One day at a time.

I drive until I find a motel. This far from the tourist traps, it's cheaper than I expected. I hand over two twenties in exchange for a room key. I almost laugh when I see room #14 is just after #12. They skipped #13. My room was supposed to be unlucky, but it suits me fine. Despite the dingy smell, I have a room. A bed to sleep in. A bathroom to use. An AC to cool the space. Even a TV to watch.

I fall back on the bed and let myself shake with giddiness.

I turn on the TV, just for the sound of it. Unpacking my duffel, I take my clothes with me into the shower. I use the soap to scrub them as clean as I can. Shirts, boxers, socks, and shorts. Then I hang them over the shower rod to dry, and let myself enjoy the water trickling over my body.

The more I scrub, the dirtier the bar of white soap becomes. The water around my feet browns. Every nook and cranny seems to hide more sediment. So I wash myself over and over. Rubbing until the water and the soap are both clean. I sit down in the shower and massage my feet. I owe them a debt. My whole life, they've helped me travel from place to place. And this summer, they carried me. I bend down and kiss each one.

My dinner is vending machine goods. Chocolate-covered donuts, snack mix, potato chips, a pack of peanuts, Kit-Kat, a can of ginger ale. I eat while watching mindless TV, and I feel like a boy again, eating junk food, sitting cross-legged in front of a screen. A rerun of *Star Trek: The Next Generation* comes on and I find myself giddy to watch a science fiction show that I grew up getting lost in.

But as Picard and the rest of the crew go up against the Borg, with the AC pushing out wintry air, and me snuggled under clean sheets and a comforter, I don't keep my eyes open for long. I sleep. Really sleep.

drive

It's ten hours from New Orleans to Abilene.

From the interstate, I watch the landscape change from swamps to forests to pastures to eventually hill country. Baton Rouge, Alexandria, Shreveport, and into Texas. Past Marshall and Longview, and into the metropolis of Dallas/Fort Worth, taking a slight detour to pass through Grapevine, where I grew up. I feel memories rushing back, and Texas welcoming me back to where I was born.

I pass Weatherford and Ranger and Baird, until finally I find myself entering the city limits of Abilene. I drive straight to my abuela's, to 1214 South Jackson Drive. Her house hasn't changed at all.

Parking my truck in front, I get out. My knees go weak. I'm not sure if it's from the long drive, or from returning here under these circumstances.

I walk up the sidewalk.

I ring the doorbell.

My stomach aches with worry.

Then Abuela opens the front door, and pushes open the screen door. She looks me over, and her hand comes up to her mouth. I've lost so much weight. My face is still bruised. But I'm here. I'm alive.

She opens her arms and steps forward. Reluctant, I step forward as well. Then she wraps her arms around me. Cool air from the house carries the scent of pine as it washes over us, as her silk blouse brushes my cheek and I bury my face into the soft skin of her neck. She smells of powder, as she always has. She kisses my ear, like she did when I was a little boy, but this time whispers, "You are safe."

And then I collapse against her.

For the first time in a long time, I do feel safe.

I am home.

AFTERWORD

It's been twenty-five years since I found myself on the streets. And you might be wondering what happened after, and what's happened since.

After I made it back to Abilene, Abuela waited patiently as I took a few days to collect myself. Then I told her that I was gay. I was terrified of how she would respond. And when I told her, she hesitated. I could see a struggle in the back of her mind. Her god or her grandson. She was only silent for a few seconds. She found a smile to offer me, a kiss on my forehead, and a voice to tell me she loved me, no matter what.

With abuela's emotional and financial help, I got into college and graduated from the University of Texas in Austin. I waited tables for a while, then moved to New York City, where I made a career out of editing and writing comics, graphic novels, and children's books. I worked at places like DC Comics and Scholastic. I worked on brands like LEGO, *Star Wars*, and *Buffy the Vampire Slayer*. I even edited several books that became *New York Times* bestsellers. Basically, I had several dream jobs.

Five years ago, I moved to Los Angeles. I got married to a wonderful man, who is one of the most incredible, kind, and compassionate people I've ever met. He accepts me with all my faults (and there are many). We have an honest, healthy relationship, and a quirky little terrier that was homeless before we adopted him. I have a wonderful relationship with my brother and his family, as well as my aunt. I also get along quite well with my in-laws. I have a wealth of great friends, a decent credit score, and a home to live in. I consider myself very lucky.

———————

As for my father?

I hated him for a few years. But Abuela often told me I only had one father and shouldn't cut him out of my life. She told me to be the bigger person. She told me if I held on to hate, it would eat me up inside. That I should forgive him.

And I did.

Though I've never been able to forget.

My dad and my stepmother ended up raising my stepsister's kids, and that experience seemed to soften my dad. He wasn't a great father, but he was a loving, kind, and even great grandparent. We still had plenty of arguments (mostly with me demanding an apology, which he refused to give). It took him time to understand that being queer wasn't something I could erase. I was born this way and it wasn't going to change. And I didn't want it to change. I liked who I'd become. I still do.

Eventually, my father accepted that I was gay, and I accepted that he would never apologize for kicking me out. After all, he thought he was doing the right thing.

After Abuela passed away in April 2022, I fell into a very dark place. She had been my parent, my support system, my guardian angel. Without her, the world felt empty and wrong and less. I felt alone.

One day, when I was feeling particularly vulnerable, I called my stepmother and father. I broke down, bursting into tears, admitting that I was struggling with life. Then my dad did something unexpected. He said he was sorry for what happened twenty-five years ago.

I didn't know how to feel. On one hand, it felt like a hug that I desperately needed, cause deep down, I'm still a little boy who wants his parents to love and take care of him. On the other hand, I've been on my own for most of my life, so I still felt abandoned, like an orphan who lost his family long ago.

Growing up, I've faced poverty, domestic violence, and time on the streets. Those events very much informed who I am now. I struggle with severe depression, anxiety, and PTSD. When triggered, I'm quick to feel rejected, terrified, and utterly alone. I spiral into dark places that last for days, weeks, or even months at a time. These kinds of emotional scars never go away. So, while I survived, a lot of me still feels broken. I found some help through therapy, medication, meditation, and exercise, among other things. And I try to think of myself as fortunate. Because I did survive. And some, maybe even many, don't.

———

So how do I go on, day-to-day?

I try to take my life philosophy from Abuela's words of wisdom: "Life is full of surprises. Some good, some bad. Some make us happier, some make us stronger, some make us wiser. We have to accept them all." No matter how hard things were for her, she always chose to focus on the good in the world. She chose to be grateful for what she had and what the universe had to offer.

These days, I try to be thankful on a daily basis. I try to write down in a journal what made today a good day. Perhaps I spent time with friends, perhaps I watched a funny movie, perhaps the sun was out, maybe I just had a cupcake. Even if it was a bad twenty-four hours, I force myself to focus on any tiny happy thing that happened. Whatever positive I can take stock of, I try to.

That often means reminding myself that my life hasn't been all bad.

My experiences have led to adventure, excitement, joy, laughter, and love. I have seen the world, found awe in small surprises, and practiced living outside of my comfort zone. I hike and bike and swim and run and read and spend time with amazing people. And I'd like to think that my queerness has given me more strength, more tolerance, more compassion, and more friendships, both inside and outside the LGBTQ+ community, than I would have had otherwise.

I have been lucky.

I have had a full life.

And my life is not over yet.